Cost and
Financial Control
for Construction Firms

Cost and Financial Control for Construction Firms

B. Cooke M.Sc., C.Eng., M.I.C.E., M.I.O.B., F.I.Q.S.,
Senior Lecturer in Building,
Stockport College of Technology

W. B. Jepson M.Sc., C.Eng., M.I.C.E.,
Professor of Construction Economics and Management,
University of Aston

First published 1979 by
THE MACMILLAN PRESS LTD
London and Basingstoke
Associated companies in Delhi Dublin
Hong Kong Johannesburg Lagos Melbourne
New York Singapore and Tokyo

Typeset in 10/11 Times Press Roman by
Reproduction Drawings Ltd, Sutton, Surrey
and printed in Great Britain by
Unwin Brothers Limited
The Gresham Press Old Woking Surrey

British Library Cataloguing in Publication Data

Cooke, Brian
    Cost and financial control for construction firms.
    1. Construction industry—Great Britain—
    Management 2. Construction industry—Great
    Britain—Finance
    I. Title II. Jepson, William Brian
    658.1'5969'0941   HD9715.G72

    ISBN 0-333-24096-0
    ISBN 0-333-24097-9   Pbk

Contents

Preface

The construction industry comprises many types of activity—design, specialist services, manufacture and production. A range of these activities is found on building projects, often undertaken on different conditions of risk and reward. The employees of most firms undertake work over a broad band of activities in the total trading situation. Financial control systems relate to firms and not just contracts. They rely on cost and income data arising from both contracts and other sources of revenue. It follows then that, although the principles and procedures of financial control need not be very different from firm to firm, cost control is likely to differ according to the nature of the activity even within firms.

The separation of responsibility for design from that for production persists. A small number of design-and-build firms and those with manufacturing interests may call for a control system directed towards the best possible product at the lowest reasonable cost. There is no generally available data base on which to raise such a system on an industry-wide basis. Were we to promote one it would be incapable of test. On the other hand, to restrict consideration to the tender and the subsequent control of contract performance would be to introduce an unrealistic and indeed illusory simplicity.

We have thus concerned ourselves with financial and cost control procedures of a kind that already exist. We have not ignored the possibility of extension or improvement, nor that a firm may be trading in building or civil engineering or as a specialist in its various parts. Because more firms appear to fail through lack of liquidity than do so by inadequacy of site control, we have set out to establish first of all the business and administrative context in which construction takes place. By so doing we take the opportunity to explore a range of terms. We then proceed to budget forecasting and the flow of funds.

The discussion of budgeting develops to include considerations of control and cash flow. The examples offered are taken from industry, as are the forms used in illustration. Cost control is then discussed in three chapters: one on monthly financial control procedures and associated tactical control options that offer themselves, another on weekly cost control procedures and a third dealing with a range of situations arising from other aspects of trade.

The potential of computer-based information systems led us to review evidence of current usage. We report the outcome. Despite outstanding instances of system development in this field there is a general picture of sluggish growth, which suggests that there is a need for some structural change.

Finally, in recognition of the increasing reference to economic and business information required of senior managers and directors, we deal with business decisions. The data to support such decisions may come, in part, from the cost and financial accounts. Certainly policy-making and its interpretation in budgeting terms are very close. It follows that investment and other time-value considerations applied to money should be discussed.

The subject matter of the book falls within the syllabus of the Final Part 2 Examination of the Institute of Building, covering aspects of the Building Production and Management Practice paper. It will also be of use to those undertaking the Institute of Quantity Surveyors' Final Examination. It should be a useful work of reference for students pursuing mid-career, undergraduate and postgraduate courses involving construction management. It is a review and a commentary rather than a manual—that may come when some greater degree of uniformity of practice exists. Those in industry should nevertheless gain from a review covering the choice and limitations of systems. By matching these to the organisation, policy and personnel of specific situations it could indeed afford a guide to action.

We are particularly grateful for the help and contribution of Carl Robinson in connection with computer systems and usage. We would also like to acknowledge with thanks the critical commentary of John Renshaw and his colleagues. In addition, however, there are the directors and executives of many firms whose contribution to research in the field, by offering their systems to review and their experience in comment, cannot be valued too highly.

B. COOKE
W. B. JEPSON

1 Introduction

Cost

The cost of anything to a consumer is what he is willing to sacrifice in cash, credit, time, effort and inconvenience to get it. The cost to a seller is the amount that he is prepared to risk in similar terms in order to trade. The cost to a maker is the sum of the various demands on resources, skill and organisation that must be met before he can offer his product to the public. Cost therefore has an objective element, which is interpreted in the context of a series of subjective judgements about risks, returns and value. It is not a single-valued function of materials, labour, plant and overheads. If it were, then the processes of costing, accounting, estimating and designing would be less of a problem.

The object of undertaking business is to gain a return for the effort. Acceptable returns are not exclusively financial but most have some form of financial expression. The direct return is read from the margin between costs and price. Cost is usually of significance not as an intrinsic value, but only in the context of the business it represents.

Faced then with the word 'cost' it is prudent to ask 'to whom and on behalf of what?' Cost control, for instance, means one thing to an architect and another to a contractor. In the former case it tends to refer to decisions affecting the geometry and detailing of works, while in the latter it is to do with timesheets and invoices; to an architect, cost control is useful in choosing between alternative design decisions, while to a contractor it is useful in decisions regarding future business tactics. Nevertheless both rely ultimately on the same input of data. Unreliable cost data lead unerringly to uncertainties in advice to designers. The priced bill submitted in support of a tender is the principal source of design-cost advice in the current U.K. situation.

Value

Value is the degree of satisfaction in some transaction, considered in relation to its cost, and involves such criteria as performance, appearance, prestige and intrinsic worth, some of which have no direct financial element. In times of financial stability, experience of price and quality over periods of time gives a sharp sense of value. Conversely uncertainties of price and quality blunt such judgements. In recent years, for instance, construction cost prediction and thus the service available to the client must have become less precise and reliable.

There are two ways in which such a decline might have been moderated—by changing the industrial structure so as to permit the direct supply of cost data from the site to the designers, or by adopting a nonfinancial unit. Work study was once thought to offer a factual basis on which to establish standards in terms of quality (materials), geometry (relationships) and time (effort), and some studies on this basis continue. The summarising capacity of finance is, however, hard to match.

A change of roles and relationships so as to obviate the 'cost-to-price' and 'price-to-cost' advice steps would call for some suppression of price competition. This is, however, the basis on which the J.C.T. form of contract is framed, and it responds very sluggishly to immediate pressures, let alone structural ones. For instance, the inequities arising from high inflation have only been moderated by an indexing procedure for cost reimbursement when the rate is in decline. Nor is effective pressure for change likely to come from the obvious quarter—the client. The industry's largest single client is the Government, and in the civil service it has no significant revolutionary cadre. Client pressure otherwise must be a minority effort.

Before we begin to use the terms that arise from contractual and administrative procedures we should discuss the manner in which construction business is conducted so that the terms may then be introduced in the context of the activities to which they refer.

The Business of Building

The client has a need for some product of construction. It is usual for him to have a site in mind or in his possession. The design and economy of construction works are strongly influenced by the site and, when considering design alternatives, it may not occur to the client that it might be better to build elsewhere. It must be remembered that the contractor is to build to instructions: a lack of wisdom in briefing, leading to inadequate or erroneous instructions, may well result in increased demands on client funds.

A client who has a site, and recognises its importance as a factor in the situation, may gain building or other construction works by a number of means.

(1)   He may simply purchase a product from a range, after inspection in prototype form; the purchase will be subject to some understanding of specification and warranty (standards of design, manufacture and assembly, and the extent of guarantee on which he can depend).

(2)   He may purchase components that are familiarly available for assembly into the product; direct labour and D.I.Y. activities fall into this category. This procedure confers flexibility in dealing with contingency events.

(3)   Specifying needs in terms of performance, he may then select from competing offers to supply a complete functioning unit.

(4)   He may enter into negotiation with a firm that will design and build, specifying needs in the process of developing a design solution. Firms offer some guarantee against excessive costs by accepting liability if increases exceed a stated sum, and such works tend to be conducted with free client access to site accounts.

(5)   He may enter into a dialogue with a professional designer, who will pre-

pare plans to form the basis on which tenders may be invited. The tenders relate to the performance of certain described work, and may be negotiated or made subject to competition.

The greater part of construction business is conducted under arrangements such as those in (5). In this case, description is crucial to the subsequent discussion and decision. Normally in the United Kingdom the quantity surveyor prepares *bills of quantity* which are descriptive of the work. Drawings and specifications are not necessarily contract documents, but misinterpretation of the bill because of failure to refer to them will gain little sympathy. Civil engineers issue bills but include drawings and specifications as contract documents and may omit the detailed description of an item and simply refer to some specific drawings or paragraphs. American practice has been to rely on drawings and specifications and to leave the billing to the builder.

For building and for civil engineering works *standard forms of contract* have come into existence. These are characterised by the variables and risks associated with their particular way of doing business. If, during construction, new facts emerge and it is required that plans should be changed in response, then it is necessary to amend the instructions to the contractor. There must be provisions to enter and account for 'variations'. The manner in which the contract provides for these differs between forms of building contract, and between building and civil engineering. Because the inclusion of certain risks within the contractor's area of liability might cause an undue inflation of price, some risks are carried by the client and a 'fluctuations' clause is included. Because *latent defects* may emerge some time after the work has been completed, it is usual for the client to retain a proportion of the sum due (known as 'retention money') until a *defects-liability period* has expired.

In alternatives (1) and (2) the client depends on his own judgement in broad areas of design and suitability. He is largely paying in advance of satisfaction. He is concerned with the warranties by which to insure himself against defective goods supplied. There are no adjustments for variations, fluctuations or retention monies in any accounting sense.

In alternative (3), apart from payments on account (which, by reducing the supplier's indebtedness during the course of the works, may reduce the over-all cost to the client), outgoings are subject to some demonstration of performance after commissioning. Some retention money may be held over for a period, but neither variations nor fluctuations are the concern of the customer.

Whereas in cases (1) and (2) such documentation as there is would be that of the suppliers, finance houses and insurance companies concerned, in case (3) there is a need for some technical and commercial draughtsmanship. The terms of the agreement may be crucial in the instance of a dispute. In cases (1) and (2) there is an open-market relationship, with open-market risks and the advantages of testing and choice, but case (3) agreement looks forward to future accomplishment and, unless both parties have entirely the same concept of the ultimate product, then realisation may not meet expectations.

Specification, which in case (3) is a matter of performance, becomes in cases (4) and (5) more a matter of condition related to elements and components. British Standard Specifications are directed to the minutiae of construction while

Codes of Practice are necessary to deal with assemblies of those elements and components. In the former case concern is with constituents, dimensions and treatment, while in the latter it is with strengths, deflections, resistance to dynamic loading, etc.

Accounting for Business

A client may pay for his building on the basis of monthly accounts. Any gains are in future returns or even in ceasing to pay rents himself. To those who serve him his payments are treated as income and their costs are the accrued expense of providing the service. Trading activity is the sum of many incomes and outgoings. The difference between trading income and expenditure is 'gross profit' and it appears in the 'trading account', which is a periodic statement of sales and the cost of those sales.

Most firms have incidental income, as from investments, and incidental outgoings in rent, commissions and the upkeep and maintenance of the firm's equipment and accommodation. These are taken into account in the 'profit-and-loss account' whose outcome is 'net profit' (or loss).

Thus far, account has been taken only of the 'net worth' or wealth of the business. Adding the value of things owed and owned at a particular date of account permits a 'balance sheet' to be drawn up. From this a measure of 'solvency' and 'liquidity' as well as of net worth can be gained. Solvency is the ability to raise cash or near-cash to meet outstanding debts. Liquidity is the ability to meet short-term demands for cash so as to pay wages and other crucial demands for payment.

Financial Performance

A firm may measure its prosperity in a number of ways. It may look favourably on an annual growth of net worth. It may seek to maintain a level of net profit from year to year. However, net worth may be increased simply by revaluing assets in response to inflation, and net profit may reflect a reluctance to undertake essential investment in assets. Therefore it is more usual to devise appropriate indices for the nature of the firm and business and to take profit, for instance, as a percentage of turnover. This relates profit to the volume of business. Profit measured against 'capital employed' (the value of assets—other than intangible ones such as valuations for goodwill—less current liabilities, that is, creditors) gives a reading of the return on investment.

It can be seen that when business ceases to represent a flow that is relatively free of abrupt interruptions or surges, but deals in items large enough momentarily to distort as assessment of turnover, then any statement of account may mislead unless it is accompanied by some attempt at reconciliation. Such a situation sometimes arises in construction: monthly financial statements covering a number of contracts may be distorted by particular events, which must be recorded as the source of the distortion. It is clear that the requirements of 'integrated accounting' for a project profit-and-loss account at the end of each accounting period may give rise to great problems of cost and value reconciliation. It is obviously important to resolve such inherent problems before considering the details of accounting procedure.

Income

In cases (3)–(5) we have to contend with income dependent on periodic contractual payments arising from *interim measurements* of completed work. Such measurements form the basis for an *interim certificate* indicating the value of work done, the amount to be withheld as retention money, and the amount of payment due (total valuation less retention and previous payments). The client may be required to pay for unfixed goods and materials (which then become his property). Payments may be made for temporary works that enable the construction to proceed. Other payments against completed work depend on the form of contract and the way in which work is billed. At the simplest it may be payment on account of some proportion of work done. On the other hand it may mean the measurement of work identified with priced items of a bill of quantities, measurement being extended by means of billed *rates* to compose a valuation.

Valuations

If the value applied to work is based on quantity 'in place' then it may not reflect the way in which costs arise in the course of the work. Some cost may have arisen against future production, as, for instance, in the provision of preliminaries or when shuttering for concrete is used and will later be re-used a number of times.

The result of successful estimating is to gain work without cutting the rates of items which are likely to involve extras or to bring in early returns. Cost–value comparisons, and particularly interim ones, may thus conceal weighting exercises. Estimators do not expect precision in the level of individual items. To base cost comparison data on the billed rates may not then yield much of direct value. Unless, indeed, the method of measurement is such that production data, through cost records, influence the estimator in pricing a bill, then a whole dimension of assumptions by architects and quantity surveyors relating to the cost planning of jobs is brought into question.

The existence of a grey area in information about cost may permit the contractor some flexibility in negotiating settlement for work done. Whether this offsets losses due to inability to relate cost feedback to price is a matter of conjecture. The fact is that civil engineers have done something to reduce the area of uncertainty because, in part, there was evidence that the time spent arguing over minor variations cost more than the benefit to be gained. Gilbreth, an early apostle of scientific management, demonstrated over 100 years ago that means existed to increase bricklayers' output by very much greater amounts than the margins that preoccupy estimators. Tools and procedures have not responded to scope for change of this order nor have outputs risen over that time. If, however, substantial variations in output are possible, and we wish to exploit cost reductions in estimating, then clearly the labelling and storage of recorded data become critical. Indeed no rational approach to the establishment of a data-processing system can usefully proceed unless fact can be directly related to associated conditions and judgements. The ground becomes treacherous. Once away from the invoice and the certificate, which contain any technical data (the responsibility of someone else), the accountant deals in abstract number. There is then a temptation to let the accounts people work on a raft of their own devising, producing their statements of account accordingly. Others manage to obtain the information that they need by means of indices and sample observations. Change to a more integrated system might arise from pressure for contributory advice by constructors. To some extent, management contracting provides a project management organisation which has access to such data.

Records

To allocate cost to activities requires that each document which relates to some *factor of production* should be labelled. The part of the cost which it represents and which is attributable to the activity is then duly charged. *Timesheets* and *plant returns* as well as invoices are involved. Clearly a delivery of sand can hardly be checked barrow by barrow, but few items serve one activity. It is necessary therefore to identify 'cost centres' which relate to activity at a level that has a recognised identity to operatives, foremen and managers. Codes are set up to label each cost centre. These must be added at the place of work where the transaction related to the document can be seen to contribute to the cost centre concerned. Often a vehicle for the action is necessary and appears in the form of, say, a *job card* or a *stores issue voucher*. Its adoption entails administrative (overhead) expense.

This is particularly so where some allocation procedure has to be set up. Bulk materials on the one hand, and the telephone or electricity accounts on the other, may be charged to several heads. Hoisting equipment and cranage are not exclusive to certain cost centres. Charges may indeed have to be allocated to some interim centre and then distributed (on the basis of some agreed formula so that similar costs on different jobs may be compared).

Time

The essence of any departure from routine accounting is the probability that a gain of information will afford benefit. In terms of control, benefit depends on an ability to act in correcting an adverse situation. We are dealing then as much with time as with data. There must be an interval between a physical stage of progress and the account that represents its financial implications. If that interval is long then it eats into the time available for any corrective action. On the other hand, if haste leads to a statement which is open to challenge, then more time is wasted establishing the true position. Control demands veracity rather than accuracy and speed rather than haste.

Job Status

After the 'practical completion' of the works inadequacies of performance are beyond remedy. There may be gains or losses to be made in agreeing the remeasurement of billed items or in negotiating variations. In terms of profit and loss the actual status of the contract emerges as negotiation for the issue of the 'final certificate' proceeds. There may also be cost implications of liability for defects over this period which eat into the outstanding retention monies. Because the retention period is long—contractually usually six months—and failure to agree may extend it, the job is long over and its staff dispersed when its status is finally declared.

Feedback

It is in the nature of construction that there is only a remote prospect of another contract being similar in type, size, timing and duration. Data that reflect abnormal conditions must not be allowed to distort records without comment. The interval before retrieval of such data may outstretch the corporate memory of the work from which they emanate. Only the data entered into the system are there to be retrieved; thus the facts that are likely to be relevant to future planners, estimators and managers must be anticipated by the designers of the accounting system or, when called on, this system may fail to perform.

The people who know what so many hours of such a quantity of material mean in operational terms are the workface supervisors. There are the signers of time-sheets, those who order up plant or materials. Many are unfamiliar with administrative procedures and feel suspicious and uneasy in dealing with them. Without a simple system, and appropriate training and encouragement, such men cannot be expected to give much beyond minimal performance. This is an important matter, which should be taken into account by firms when making provision for the training of their personnel.

The Human Factor

The accounting system itself simply creates machinery. In human terms, the contributions that determine its effectiveness are conditioned by the choice of the system and the role that each person involved—from directors to workface supervisors—sees that it requires him to play.

Those who see no special benefit arising from their contribution are unlikely to give it much thought and care. If the input to any system is unreliable, either by witting manipulation or by error, then its output must suffer.

Accounting Terms

The standard against which performance is to be measured is contained in a 'budget statement'. The system of 'management by objectives' seeks to identify the target performance for each of its sections (and thus their managers) as part of that statement.

Forecasts of income and expenditure from the various parts of a firm are brought together, aggregated and then possibly amended to produce a plan that seeks to meet business objectives making the best use of available resources. The 'budget' is a financial statement of this plan. It thus embraces not only the objectives outlined in its preparation but a number of others implicitly reflected in the submissions and any vote involved in its adoption. Some of these implied objectives may be personal to its directors, and indeed the budget must reflect them, lest those in authority lean their influence towards decisions that depart from the plan.

We have already dwelt on costing, the general allocation and analysis of expenditure with regard to various contracts, services, processes and activities undertaken in pursuit of enterprise. *Cost analysis* implies the definition of elements such that information can be applied across intervals of time to work of a

similar nature. *Cost control* implies the gathering of information on the basis of
which the need for action to alter or remedy the observed performance may be
evaluated and the most appropriate type of action determined.

When it is necessary to provide comparative data, then the form that these take
must be properly understood. A *spot cost* is the product of limited observation and
measurement of cost factors affecting an activity in specific circumstances. *Unit
costs* express the recorded expenditure per unit quantity of output— cost per cubic
metre of excavation, etc. Again, if too general a set of data is considered, very significant variations due to circumstances may be missed, and the description of the
unit quantity is particularly important. *Standard costs* refer to the expected output or consumption of a defined process in stated conditions. Construction processes suffer uncertainties as a result of which a range of values will arise from like
observations spread over different sites and time, and some statistical techniques
could help in considering such values.

Words like 'loss' may be used in an interim sense, which is likely to mislead. A
deficit is bound to occur when working under J.C.T. contract conditions over some
period. Let us take the case of a contract worth £X000 of duration Y months. If
the value of the work done were to accumulate at a constant rate then its cumulative value at any time would be that shown at the appropriate month by the dashed
line in figure 1.1. In fact there is a period in which the work is built up and organ-
ised. It could well be restricted by the absence of services or access, or in piling or
other works. Equally, finishing off and tidying up is part of a tailing-off process.
The cumulative value of work done is then more likely to be represented by the
continuous curve. From its shape it is known as an S curve. Since examples of
this curve will occur in later chapters, a more detailed discussion of this curve is
worth while.

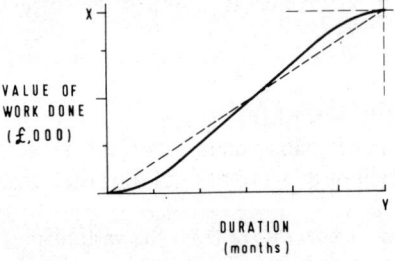

Figure 1.1

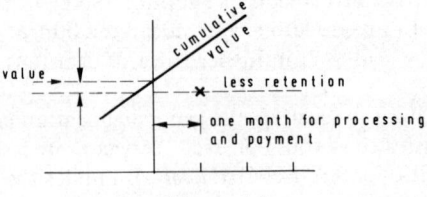

Figure 1.2

If the value figures are agreed, then income follows only after a deduction of retention money and a delay for processing and payment. Figure 1.2 illustrates the effect, and the continuous curve in figure 1.3 shows its completed form, assuming a constant deduction percentage up to physical completion (*Y*), when half of the retention is returned and a defects-liability period of six months is assumed.

Cost accumulates in a different way. Some smaller payments go on all the time, some (such as wages) are paid weekly and most of the personal accounts, including salaries, are paid monthly. Materials are a substantial part of the job cost and fall into the latter category. Figure 1.4 illustrates in a simplified form how cost accumulates, and after further simplification a cumulative cost curve should look like figure 1.5.

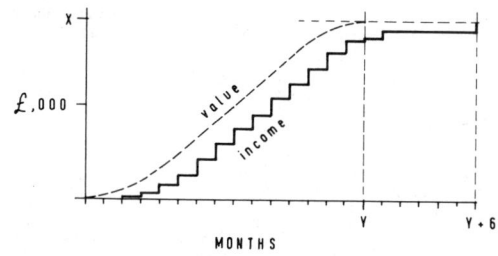

Figure 1.3

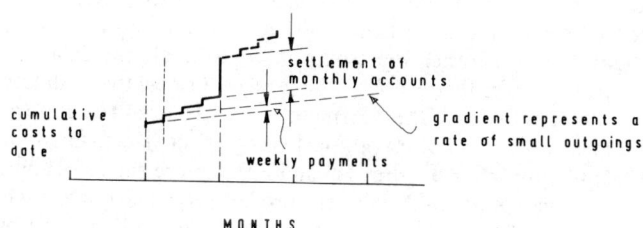

Figure 1.4

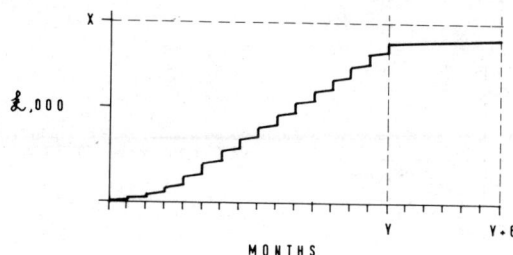

Figure 1.5

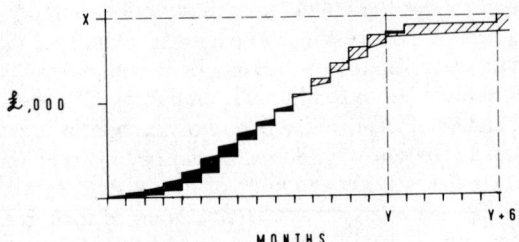

MONTHS

Figure 1.6

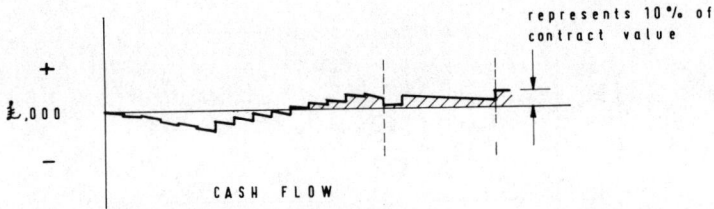

CASH FLOW

Figure 1.7

Putting figures 1.3 and 1.5 together we have a period in which the cost exceeds income, blocked in black, and one in which income exceeds cost, hatched. It could well be that some month starts in credit and ends in debit before the next income payment. Figure 1.6 then represents at any ordinate the balance of cash flow. This is represented in figure 1.7 by the positive or negative ordinates derived from figure 1.6. In this instance the contractor ceases to need to support the job with capital some six months before physical completion. The ultimate return is about 10 per cent of turnover. Figures 1.8 and 1.9 explore the effect on cash flow of an outcome of 5 per cent and $2\frac{1}{2}$ per cent respectively. The curve rotates about its origin and the effect is to reduce the recovery of funds in later months, and to prolong the period in which the contractor must finance the work. Therefore, a 'loss' in month 3 is not the same thing as a loss in the later months, and simply to report it is pointless. However, to compare actual and planned cash flow positions, at first an attractive idea, is to compare an outcome derived from judgements and

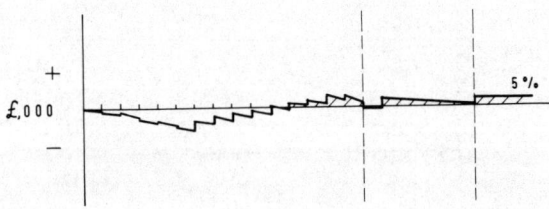

Figure 1.8

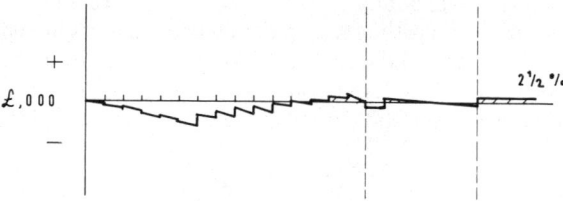

Figure 1.9

activities by many different people. An actual cash flow balance fluctuates very much more than the idealised cases in figure 1.7 and to act on a single adverse result might be imprudent, while the next one, being a further month away, could be too late. The alternative is to establish cost standards of performance at a more detailed level and to report on these in addition to the over-all status of the contract.

Alternative Procedures

It is clear that such a further breakdown cannot extend to the detail of items in the bills of quantity. Quite apart from the dubious relationship of estimators' rates to operational performance, there would be too much information to cope with at a time. Repetitive work, however, lends itself to a breakdown by 'stages' and in housing contracts there is often provision for stage payments. Provided such business is likely to continue then a procedure can centre around a standard series of stages, and target prices can be set out for each. For the once-off, architect-designed, competitive tender type of job the difficulty would be to identify stages that would permit comparisons between different jobs and at different times. The Ministry of Education introduced elemental billing some years ago, in response to the need for cost feedback to the designer of schools. The R.I.C.S. Cost Advisory Service has adopted a standard set of elements and collects unit costs for the same purpose, over a range of building types. Unfortunately, the same breakdown cannot be so readily adapted to tendering or production requirements as can alternative forms and, once again, the data depend on price rather than cost.

It must be in the interests of easy reconciliation to bill work so that price reflects the way in which cost actually accrues. Skoyles' campaign in this cause, centred on the Building Research Establishment, is well known. Operational bills group items into stages of work, thus trades appear under several heads rather than one and the bill is longer, and before enquiries can go to potential subcontractors their work has to be extracted and regrouped. Hence, a tool suited to improved pricing and certification is less suited for the primary purpose of such documents, namely, to act as a vehicle for contractor selection.

It can be argued with some justificatijon that billing by trades for simplicity in tendering, by elements for simplicity in cost planning or by operational criteria for simplicity in dealing with cost feedback to estimators and in reconciliation and certification is simply an alternative arrangement of the same data. A well-designed system could then process the data on demand in whatever way proved best. We explore such a possibility later, in considering computers.

This introduction sets out to establish the business centres in which construction exercises of financial and cost control take place, and also to bring to the reader's attention some of the terms which are commonly used. The following two chapters develop this process and extend its detail.

2 Costs, Control and Construction

Resources are required to promote, achieve and control the activities of an enterprise. Control is the process of regulation which seeks to maintain conformity to some plan. Those who are responsible for the execution of the plan must be aware of the objectives on which it is based, and the resources at their disposal may be materials, services, skills, energy, information and working capital. All of these give rise to costs, either in their intrinsic worth or in procuring, processing or controlling them. Equally, it is rare not to state some objectives in terms of a financial outcome. Consequently money is often the most convenient common unit for inputs, outputs and outcomes, and provides the means of reducing a complex process to a single value such as profit.

Some outcomes involve subjective factors or lie in the future, and lend themselves less readily, if at all, to statement in financial terms. For instance, it is difficult to show a payment that is made in the interests of goodwill, and may bring substantial benefit, as anything but a loss. Just as a total concern for financial factors can mislead, so the capacity of financial descriptions to summarise large amounts of information should not be allowed to obscure the need to go back into the detail of the matter for explanations. Finance is useful for reporting situations but any attempt to review their causes may well expose its limitations.

Short-lived repetitive processes can be reviewed and refined. The time taken by a cycle of activities or the proportion of rejects may be monitored so as to provide an adequate index of performance by means of which it may be controlled. Construction takes the process to the materials rather than the materials to the process, and even repetitive activities are influenced by changes of weather and location. There are practical problems in deciding what is to be controlled and in what terms. Control itself costs money, since it is grafted on to a process in order to monitor and regulate it. The value of control is then expressed by the effectiveness of that regulation in the short term, and also the reliability with which future operations can be forecast.

Construction extends from simple works of shelter to the regulation of the forces of nature. The site on which the work is carried out has a unique influence on its character, and the location, the season and the workforce are different for each specific project. Experience is among the most important resources of any firm and is particularly important in the realistic establishment of objective standards. Cost control in construction therefore demands a detailed understanding of both organisation and technical content, which, if supported by an effective information system, must reduce uncertainty and thus risk.

Accounts

There are many means by which the acquisition and development of resources are recorded, but the summarisation of this information into a statement of site status always involves accounting.

In seeking information from such accounts we ask broadly two kinds of question

(1)   those concerned with the routine administration of receipts and payments, with assets and liabilities, and with liquidity, solvency and the ever-present responsibilities of business; and

(2)   those concerned with the state of the enterprise, comparing plan with performance, so that we may initiate any corrective action required.

The former are the product of routine (subjective) accounts and the latter of additional accounts set up to monitor performance in relation to specific objectives.

Corrective action is called for not only in its short-term or tactical sense, but in the long term to adjust strategy. If the cost of establishing control has to be justified in terms of direct savings or reduced risks, then many benefits lie so far in the future as to make any valuation of benefit somewhat speculative. A great part of the potential benefits lies in the retrieval of useful information by managers, planners, estimators and others, and more may be derived if designers and their financial advisors are able to gain access.

It follows that control arising from subjective accounts is limited but cheap, and that the utility of objective accounts and thus the cost of maintaining them is unlikely to be justified under conditions of restricted use and access. Access depends, however, on the form in which information can be made available. As will be seen later, the form and regulation of the input data are crucial.

Transactions

Accounts are the record of the enterprise in terms of the deployment of its financial resources. These start with transactions, which arrange themselves in a more or less random manner. The general sequence of events necessitates them but the exigencies of manufacture, delivery, availability and so on determine their incidence. Records of transactions must start with their receipt, and the routines by which receipts are acknowledged and entered into the system assume great importance. They label and direct the documentary evidence of the transaction to the corresponding accounts and, indirectly, to the information from which the employment of the resources will be monitored.

Book-keeping

Book-keeping is the routine of classification, labelling and processing to which transactions are subject. It recognises the two parties to a transaction, that one gives and the other receives, and that from one point of view the gain is in goods or services and from the other the gain is in money. Accounts are thus like a sheet of glass: the way in which entries appear depends on which side you stand. Accountants have to be consistent so that, as their records are periodically summed and balanced, they readily disclose any amounts owed or owing and to whom. There are *personal accounts* for each firm or person with whom the enterprise has business. Their object is just those statements of account by which to arrange settlements. In addition *real accounts* are needed to account for states of ownership; — the purchases, sales, machinery and buildings that permit the enterprise to continue — an account of which is periodically necessary. *Nominal accounts* are maintained so that the situation in respect of predictable areas of apportionment of income or expenditure can be made clear on demand. In order to make periodic statements to directors, managers, shareholders and others the foregoing accounts are summarised and aggregated into trading accounts, profit-and-loss accounts, and balance sheets. The accountant is then concerned with cost as a component of a series of balances of inflows and outflows. The manager's need to know where things are going wrong is not considered unless specifically requested. A conscious and planned isolation of costs from accounts becomes necessary if control is intended beyond that directly attributable to the routine administration of business.

As routine accounting is the essential element of a set of procedures that can be adapted to wider needs, it tends to establish the general form and structure. Often the pressure of necessity causes it to be created before any serious consideration has been given to the ways in which the data that it contains can be further employed. Accounting information is classified on input by posting it to appropriate ledger accounts. These are identified by ledger folio numbers. At the end of each accounting period a balance is struck and an account is submitted for payment. The headings of real or nominal accounts are derived from the items in periodic statements of profit-and-loss accounts or balance sheets. That a purchase increases the company's stock of fixed assets would, for instance, be of relevance in such circumstances.

On the other hand, should managers wish to know what return they are getting from an investment, then, quite apart from generating a demand for further information (about such things as running costs, outputs and possibly location), this requires the retrieval of the data for secondary processing. If such information is likely to be needed frequently, then the data should be given a reference *at the time of input*; this will facilitate its retrieval. Such secondary classifications tend to be specific to the particular enterprise, and call for technical or commercial knowledge of the firm beyond that obvious to those who normally undertake routine book-keeping.

Since it is the technical and managerial staff who find themselves involved in accounting when accounts acquire an objective function, it will be useful here to summarise some of the basic facts about book-keeping.

Book-keeping Procedures

In any transaction the firm (the body conducting the enterprise concerned) may be involved in one of two capacities.

(1)   The firm receives cash or credit and a double entry results. In this case, the account *describing* the *nature* of the receipt (sales, purchase returns, etc.) is *credited*, and the account *identifying* the *origin* of the receipt (cash, bank, customer, etc.) is *debited*.

(2)   The firm *pays* or gives credit and a double entry results. In this case, the account *describing* the *purpose* of the payment (purchases, travelling, rates etc.) is *debited*, and the account *identifying* the *beneficiary* of the payment (creditor, bank, etc.) is *credited*.

The document representing the transaction, often an invoice, must provide

(a)   the names and addresses of both parties;
(b)   the description of goods or services – number, unit price, total, trade discount and identity (catalogue number or description);
(c)   the terms of the transaction (discount for cash within 30 days, etc.).

If objective accounting procedures are also envisaged then some code or annotation must be added *before* the invoice is passed for processing, or otherwise its retrieval at a later stage may be very time-consuming. This code represents the allocation of the goods, services or money to *cost centres* (representing processes, areas of activity that occur over a number of processes, machines or shops undertaking a particular process or conversion, etc.). Then, when the cost attributed to a specific period of activity with respect to a cost centre is required, the sum can be retrieved by reference to the code.

Manual data processing creates a ledger folio number under which to gain information for each purpose. Additional work (and thus cost) arises from pressure to proliferate such ledger accounts. Mechanical data processing becomes necessary as complexity grows.

The administration of an enterprise gives rise to overhead costs, which may be a significant factor in a firm's competitiveness. Better utilisation of sources of data is a worthy aim, whereas to allow new and independent information procedures to be set up can be wasteful.

Effectiveness

Complexity induces difficulty and even error in the classification of transactions. Resources deployed expressly to produce quantities of information may give little return if much of it is simply held in the remote possibility of need, or is applied only for the benefit of low-grade decision-making. With mechanical data storage and retrieval facilities a well-controlled input, accurately labelled, can generate answers on demand and in a specified form. By monitoring the working of the system the investment in processing time can be related to the benefit gained from its output. Check procedures built into the system can save time in locating and correcting errors, reconciling differences, and discounting information that does not meet specified statistical standards of probability. Using information without recognition of its in-built uncertainties, offering information in terms other than those required by the user and providing information too late all depress its value, even to zero.

The documents upon which the accuracy of data input depends are the responsibility of the initiating organisation and those members of a firm's staff who receive, check, allocate and certify the disposition of goods or services. Only after passing through their hands does an item enter the accounting system and, however good this is, it is no better than its input. Such systems are indeed operated in isolation, the appropriate magnitude and any addresses may be beyond the knowledge of those who carry out the system's routine operations.

Routine

By way of an example let us consider (say) the delivery of windows to a site.

A schedule of window types and numbers should be part of the working drawings. The schedule has to be checked against the drawings and, after resolving any queries, the order may be placed.

The timing and sequence of deliveries for installation can minimise double handling, storage and protection costs, and thus a call-up schedule based on the over-all order is a site responsibility additional to that which is the basis for purchasing.

The manufacturer, unless he is dealing with standard types produced for stock and shelved until required, tends to produce batches by type. Production timing and sequence thus tends to differ from the call-up schedule. To save warehousing, storage, double handling and the organisational costs of facilitating phased deliveries to schedule, the manufacturer favours large loads transported as produced. It is easier to check a schedule that you have yourself originated. An apparent price benefit at the quotation stage can be lost in overheads arising from delivery policy and practice, not all of which can be laid at the door of the supplier. It should be made clear when loads are intended for direct distribution on site.

Misunderstandings arising from the definition of cost centres may, if they lead to incorrect or inconsistent allocations, distort the aggregates and balances of the reports that result. In our case we must know if 'windows' are separate from exterior walls, and if so whether the cost centre is to include glazing, fixing pads or clamps, bedding sills, etc. Perhaps the distribution costs of hoisting and carrying are to be separately identified and included. Whatever the definition, not only materials but men's time, equipment costs and consumables must be allocated to the cost centre, and this involves checkers, timekeepers, foremen and others, all of whom must understand their responsibilities within the system.

The illustration has so far concerned itself only with site staff. Having certified and coded the invoice that is sent to site for the purpose they return it to the accounts department, and headquarters staff become involved.

The invoice will have been checked against the order before passing it to site (some firms do not give priced bills and invoices to site staff). On return, duly certified and addressed, the document reaches entry in the journal and is later posted to an appropriate account. There is a known commitment before this time, and some firms price the delivery slip from the records of the order and make reconciling adjustments when full information is forthcoming. If this is not done then any comparison of cost against the value of work done calls for considerable work of reconciliation or is of dubious value.

The firm's accounts may provide ledger folio numbers for general accounts such as 'purchases' or 'joinery'. Some may have job accounts subdivided into the factors of production, one of which will be materials. For general routine accounting purposes little more is needed, and indeed any proliferation could introduce inaccuracies in posting entries. However, to relate entries to site control activity calls for more detailed addressing in order that data can be retrieved and related to cost centres. This tends to be a separate and additional exercise, and routine book-keeping checks restrict themselves to posted entries. The invoice is checked against the order. The details of actual delivery are certified by site staff. Periodic trial balances check that both parts of a double entry correspond. Auditors check for complete omission of items or the inclusion of fictitious entries. Where the covering order provides for materials to be called up by site then there will be a ceiling quantity which, if exceeded, requires explanation. There may be a periodic check that accounts qualifying for cash discounts are cleared in time.

Other materials present different problems. The manner in which bulk materials are actually utilised is rarely subject to control; thus to allocate their cost to cost centres involves an exercise in apportionment that may be somewhat subjective. Also, materials that are held in stock after delivery can only be made subject to account if issues are documented. True objective cost control thus requires the existence of procedures for materials control. In countries where most materials are imported or involve difficulties of procurement such control is likely to exist. The U.K. construction industry, on the other hand, has been orientated towards plant and labour, and there is a limit to the overheads expenditure arising from control procedures that can be justified.

It is argued that labour and plant are the variables that site staff can regulate and that, given expert purchasing by headquarters staff, and security and tidiness at site, losses are not likely to justify materials-control costs. On the other hand, research into materials wastage frequently discloses levels in excess of 'estimators' allowances.

Those in charge of construction have to decide whether what they want is cost control, or labour-and-plant cost control, or financial control with random cost checks by special study.

Control

The word 'control' implies that judgement is exercised to regulate performance in the execution of some plan. Objectives must be clearly understood and articulated. Standards must be stated in terms of some unit that is both appropriate and measurable. Inept regulation may disrupt control.

The classic analogy is that of the governor of an engine, which responds to an excess shaft speed by reducing the power input, and to declining shaft speed by increasing power input. If the regulation of power is too crude then the engine 'hunts' between a state of excess and insufficiency and fails to settle to the uniform speed intended. Thus, there are degrees of effectiveness of control, and those of an acceptable kind are demonstrated by conformity with plan.

There are three elements of a control process

(1) A *detector* acknowledges stated standards of performance (although these may be subject to periodic review), stated in measurable units, and monitors the output of a process in terms of these standards. Within acceptable limits of deviation nothing further is required, but if any deviation passes beyond these limits then it is part of the detector's function to initiate a signal.

(2)   A *system of communication* provides the means for the signal to be transmitted in undistorted form. To take a simple mechanical example, the warning light on a vehicle dashboard appears as the result of an unacceptably large temperature rise.

(3)   A *reactor* responds to the signal by initiating some regulatory action to correct the situation.

It is clear that the speed of response depends on the latter two elements, and the discriminatory nature of the response of the reactor. The speed of response should be rapid in relation to the rate at which an unacceptable deviation may become critical. Furthermore it is obvious that if any element is effectively absent — as in the case of a defective warning light, or an operator whose attention is distracted — then *control does not exist.* Most systems have a back-up provision of (say) audible as well as visual warning, or warnings directed to more than one sensor. If standards only partially represent effective performance, or have become less relevant than they were, the control system itself becomes only partially effective. If the cost of maintaining control exceeds the losses at risk then the system cannot be justified.

Control systems directed to administrative processes are particularly prone to weaknesses arising from human failings. According to Bernard (1938), the 'fine art' of decision-making consists in refraining from

(a)   decisions that others should make;
(b)   decisions that cannot be made effective;
(c)   premature decisions; and
(d)   decisions on questions that have ceased to be pertinent.

However, these are rules applying to a badly designed control system. In a properly designed system there should be no doubt as to who is responsible for reaction in any given situation and irrelevant regulation should not warrant a warning. Overreaction causes a system to 'hunt', and reference to irrelevant standards is obviously pointless. Unfortunately, whereas a mechanical process that goes out of control is stopped, or breaks down, an administrative process can bumble on while individuals perform routine but pointless functions. The output of an administrative process is less easily defined for control purposes.

When the output of a process can be monitored but is such that deviation beyond some limit discounts the value of the whole operation, the reaction at that extreme stage is to abort the process. Clearly in such cases the aim of operational control is to maintain performance within warning limits, and possibly to have automatic fall-back to emergency reactor mechanisms if deviations go beyond warning limits. In an administrative context this involves a transfer of decision-making responsibility, at some point, to more senior levels of management. The over-all policy-making body for the enterprise must thus take upon itself the design of the general system of control. This body alone can state its aims and objectives in such a way that the limits of acceptability of performance become clear and it alone can identify satisfaction in terms of the cost–benefit equation. Although the detailed design of systems can be left to specialists it is unlikely that a coherent system will result from some amalgam of sectional effort; yet, in practice such a design procedure is not unusual.

Finally there is the problem arising from the need to interpret the more complicated signals generated by a control system. The red light or siren may alert an operator but leave him to investigate the situation for himself and then decide on appropriate action. The document that is intended to serve as a guide may not help in this respect. Often those to whom it is directed have no training in the evaluation and interpretation of such documents. Responsibility lies heavily on those who are expected to react to confused signals. One experienced site manager left construction for his own business when his boss berated him for 'losing money' on a contract that returned 9% rather than 10% on turnover (though at the time of contract adjudication 10% had been a higher margin than normal).

Construction

In introducing this chapter we noted some of the uncertainties and interdependences that influence construction work. The terms of accounting are common to many sorts of enterprise, and the interpretation of financial reports calls for judgement and familiarity with the conditions of the industrial or commercial process under review. Cost is incurred in the pursuit of some return or value, which depends on the degree of satisfaction with the outcome. Both cost and return tend to be specific to a particular type of activity or enterprise, and in construction there is sometimes no direct relation between the two.

The production activity that seeks to satisfy customer demand is in the hands of a contractor in most cases. The greater part of marketing — and certainly the creative part — often lies in the hands of the (separately commissioned) design organisation. The contract is then to manufacture and assemble a product designed on commission. The basis of payment to designers has its origins in a form of patronage, while that to contractors is strictly commercial. The client makes payments both under contract and in design fees. Here we are concerned only with the former. Standard forms of contract try to establish a fair apportionment of the risk but, as in the inflation of the mid-70s, some risks can escalate. The management and evaluation of outcomes is simple if performance is demonstrated on completion or delivery. If, however, ability to anticipate outcome develops only as the work progresses, then procedures to deal with fluctuations and contingencies arise, and accounting for these procedures necessarily complicates the assessment of the status of a contract as it proceeds.

Within the terms of the contract there are rated and billed items to which periodic measurement can be referred. Some variations can be valued by reference to such rates.

There are many other less significant sources of income, some of which will be discussed. Valuation involves an exercise of judgement and sometimes compromise between representatives of the client and contractors. If the outcome is prejudiced towards either generosity or parsimony, then an interim comparison of value against cost is misleading by the amount of bias involved (the following month may well see it corrected).

Variations may be treated as dayworks, which differ in nature from billed works, or, because of the conditions appertaining, cannot be rated in the same terms as similar work in the bill (that is where the estimator's assumptions at the time of estimating clearly differ from actuality). In effect, and within the guidance of agreed schedules, such works are a claim against the contingency provisions of the contract, demand additional resources and are separately accounted.

Dayworks are generally believed to be more costly than negotiated work based on a variation order, and much time may be spent agreeing a formula by which a quantity of work may be converted into a sum for payment. Negotiation may be particularly prolonged where delays or out-of-phase working have involved time-dependent costs and no comparative increase in quantity has occurred. It is then easier to make allowance for cost commitments that have already been acknowledged than to decide the provisional amount to enter against income, and a tendency to pessimism (although it might seem prudent to the quantity surveyor), may, if taken over a number of variations, conceal realisable assets.

Preliminary items that cover the provision of offices, site access, transport, hoardings, the maintenance of plant, small tools, temporary supplies of water and power, etc., are only recoverable in the basis of an agreed apportionment according to the progress of the contract. Others, such as the cost of holiday stamps, pension, travelling time, sickness, redundancy and pension payments, etc., are recovered, according to the method of their incorporation in the estimate, either by reference to the number and character of the labour force or through the labour element of rated items. In either case they contain an element of risk which represents the deviation of site conditions from the historic norm values experienced by the firm. Unless feedback data about preliminaries are available to estimators, the deviation of estimate and actuality may exceed the variations of margin being applied by the firm, in the belief that it is influencing the competitiveness of a tender.

Other apportionments correspond to allowances for attendance upon suppliers and subcontractors whose quotations are incorporated into the bill as prime cost sums. Sundry receipts may accrue from interest on suspense accounts for future liabilities. Along with discounts and sales of equipment these arise from matters of commercial judgement and procedure; they are rarely critical.

Just as we can expect that at any time there are unrealised liabilities and assets, deviations in the order of which arise partly from the nature of construction and the contractual forms adopted in that field, so equally there are factors influencing a statement of cost.

Cost must often be met before value is verified. There may be future replacement or remedial work outstanding and no more income to cover it. Quotations may not extend to the duration of the contract and, in some cases, may be subject to irrecoverable fluctuations. Again, in an accounting sense, costs do not appear as soon as a liability is assumed. There may be considerable delay in the submission and verification of an account. At any time the reported cost may differ appreciably from true current commitments. There may also be a difference in the cost – value comparison arising from an interval between the date of the accounting period and the date of valuation for the certification of progress.

In this situation considerations of tactical and sectional benefit appear. It may be argued that the firm or the individual will gain by delaying settlement. However, unless such policy intervention is recognised and recorded in the firm's confidential reports, there is considerable scope for misinterpretation. It has been suggested that, when interest rates are high, the cheapest form of finance consists of the involuntary loans of suppliers awaiting payment.

Construction has apparently adopted forms of contractual association that lack assurance and precision at interim points of a long-term process. Accordingly, any system of cost control demands a great deal of forethought in its design, if it is not to be subject to protracted procedures for reconciliation, or reliable only after such a time that tactical action has become relatively ineffective. An understanding of this point is essential to any discussion of the subject.

References

Bernard, C. I., *The Environment of Decision. The Functions of the Executive* (Harvard University Press, Cambridge, Mass., 1938).

3   Costs, Control and Companies

A board of directors, being responsible to shareholders for the financial outcome of its enterprise, must report periodically. In order to do so, it must be able to identify sources of profit and loss, and, if there is a matter at issue, to account for these profits and losses. This can, of course, be done retrospectively by initiating a detailed enquiry. Lessons are then available for incorporation into company policy, but such an enquiry may also be the occasion for action against some scapegoat, a decline in confidence on the part of the market, the resignation of experienced members of the firm and so on. It would clearly be better to introduce a form of control that would allow undesirable trends to be corrected as the particular enterprise proceeds.

A draft budget for some future period can be prepared by forecasting the outcome of current and predicted work. This may raise doubts about the continuing validity of current policy or, more specifically, may permit consideration to be given to action to provide for periods of deficit or for the deployment of surpluses. In seeking answers the board has the power to manipulate a number of variables and, having reformulated its policy, encapsulated in a budget, it can issue to those responsible for the firm's activity a statement of financial objectives against which performance may be compared. Deviations from plan can then be checked at each accounting period.

Income in construction is largely determined by interim and final valuations. These are factual and immediate. Payment has contractual safeguards. Only the product of over- or undervaluation and any matters under negotiation — as variations or claims — require review should the value of work done be questioned. Cost, on the other hand, is composed of many small items and is rarely bound in contractual terms for the period of the contract. It is subject to market forces, to additions arising from site handling and storage of materials, labour relations, problems of site and season and indeed the effectiveness of management. Payment for labour is made weekly, for subcontract work monthly under contract, but for materials against monthly account. Supplier's credit may be cheap source of finance, and the accountant has available for manipulation a substantial part of the outgoings. There may then be a marked difference between the amount of liabilities accrued and the payments in respect of them.

In order to judge the status of a contract it is desirable that the datum for any comparison should be such that progress in relation to it is readily reconciled with figures for value and cost. Weekly wages may overlap accounts due by the calendar month. Some overheads accounts are quarterly, while others — such as interest on capital employed — are levied retrospectively. We deal with adjustment later.

Finance, as we have said, is a summarising medium. It states a situation but may not offer enlightenment as to its causes. Contract cost is an aggregate of labour, materials, plant and overheads. Standards of expenditure against each of these heads, or some of them, may offer partial explanations when records of planned and actual value and cost are compared. It might be argued that sound management and good housekeeping are reflected in other ways — by a tidy site, low figures for wastage, high output per man, etc. Given strict supervision, it may then be enough in all but exceptional cases, to limit control of production, in financial terms, simply to a comparison of planned and actual valuation. Paying for insurance against remote risks may be an expensive luxury.

Construction companies promote and maintain production on a series of contracts of varying size, type and location. Each requires its own sequence of trade and equipment inputs. Where, as in the United Kingdom, payment for work done is in arrears, the firm finances at least the early stages of a contract and often all of it, until retention monies are released on physical completion. Work is obtained in competition in most cases, thus, success is not assured and the mix and timing of workload depend on circumstances outside the control of the firm. The aggregate demand on resources — finance, skilled labour, equipment — is then subject to peaks and troughs. Smoothing one demand may exacerbate the extremes of another. Managers have to be aware of all the variables whereas the accountant can concentrate on one.

Few companies have so many contracts that each is an insignificant element of the total picture. Whereas manufacturing industry can perhaps visualise its expenditure and return as a flow of varying volume, and thus can establish a manufacturing and distributing cost that breaks even for some market price of its product, construction offers no such simple index. There is apparently no alternative to a periodic budget, taking all known factors and a great deal of speculation into account, and then a process of comparison with actual performance. The period covered by a plan and the period over which standards remain valid are not the same.

Budgets

At any time a budget must project likely events in respect of

(1) work completed and awaiting settlement of the final account;
(2) work in progress;
(3) work obtained but not started;
(4) work forecast on the basis of the firm's marketing effort;
(5) work needed in order to make more effective use of company resources (that is, new directions of marketing effort).

Uncertainty increases from (1) to (5). Business forecasts may be valid for a very short time. On the other hand performance is only monitored monthly when it depends upon agreed valuations. We are thus faced with contracts of a duration extending into years, which are budgeted for hardly less than a year ahead and monitored monthly, and it is to be expected that some updating of the budget will take place. Some firms do three-monthly updates and others six-monthly updates. There is no reason why, with sophisticated data processing, it should not be done monthly *providing* the input is reliable. This is the usual weak point: almost all managers, when faced with an unfavourable report, first go to check the input.

Forecasting Cost

Contracts that are in progress not only have documents in the form of programmes, materials schedules, payroll records, etc., but have behind them the realisation of risk and the probability of profit. What remains to be done thus includes less uncertainty. There is considerable work in forecasting future cost but the data exist upon which to base the process. If the site maintains a record of deliveries, invoiced services and subcontractor progress, it can apply a rate to most of them and arrive at a figure for total liabilities. This can be reconciled with payments made, and discrepancies can be entered after clarification. If this is not done then a monthly report of cost based upon accounts paid may be both difficult to reconcile with any particular stage of progress and may be regarded on site simply as the somewhat dubious report of an outside agency.

Contracts obtained but only in the early stages of execution again have a programme and documents based on quantities and, if the programme is sufficiently detailed, forecasts of labour and plant requirements. Once again, a cost forecast is clearly possible, if sufficient time is invested.

Contracts in prospect may be identified by little more than a broad description of the work, a contract sum and a contract duration. Some may have a declared starting date, but in other cases even this may be no more than speculation. When tendering for such work, however, the net cost estimate is adjudicated and a tender price emerges. The difference between the estimated net cost and the price represents a margin to compensate for perceived areas of special risk and to afford an appropriate return to the company. Cost should then equate to value less margin if the estimator is right. Figure 3.2 represents the cost accumulation for margins of 0, 5, 10 and 15 per cent; we will discuss the form of the curve in more detail later. As durations may be in months or years the chart has a percentage basis but figure 3.3 permits conversion.

Clearly some contracts do better and some worse than hoped. The risk may prove different from that for which the adjudicators provided. Budgetary planning permits a forecast of possible peaks and troughs in monthly income and expenditure. Its effectiveness depends on the validity of the model. An empirical approach might be to record the cost–value position at stated intervals through groups of contracts for work of a type of activity. It should then be possible to forecast future work of a similar kind, by the use of Monte Carlo simulation techniques, (see Singh, 1968).

This procedure affords values that incorporate the statistical probability of a deviation from the mean. Data would have to be collected specifically for the purpose. The outcome is no more than speculative, however it is gained.

Research has suggested that there is some appropriate form of S-curve geometry for specific types of work (see Hardy, 1970). The form used in figure 3.1 is adopted herein. It has no special virtue apart from its simplicity, and the readiness with which it can be produced. One quarter of the cumulative value

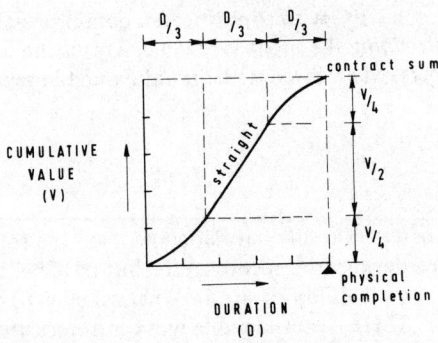

Figure 3.1

occupies a build-up period of one third of the contract duration, and a further quarter occupies the tail-off period of one-third. Half of the accumulated value is gained over a centre third of steady progress. In the cases illustrated a parabolic curve, drawn freehand, links the centre section to the origin and end.

Although we introduce it to examples that refer to site control, this function would only occur in conditions based on a more factual curve. The sum of forecast incomes and outgoings some months ahead is so speculative as to be adequately derived from the simple form, however. As the contract becomes more immediate the S-curve can be developed directly from forecast progress and the plans for the work. For a contract in the somewhat remote future, the forecast must suffer updating at least once and any discussion of alternative S-curve geometries only refers to the difference between approximations (see Nisbet, 1973).

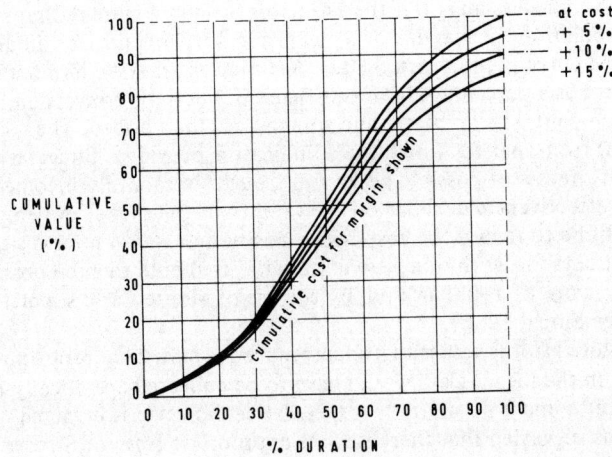

Figure 3.2

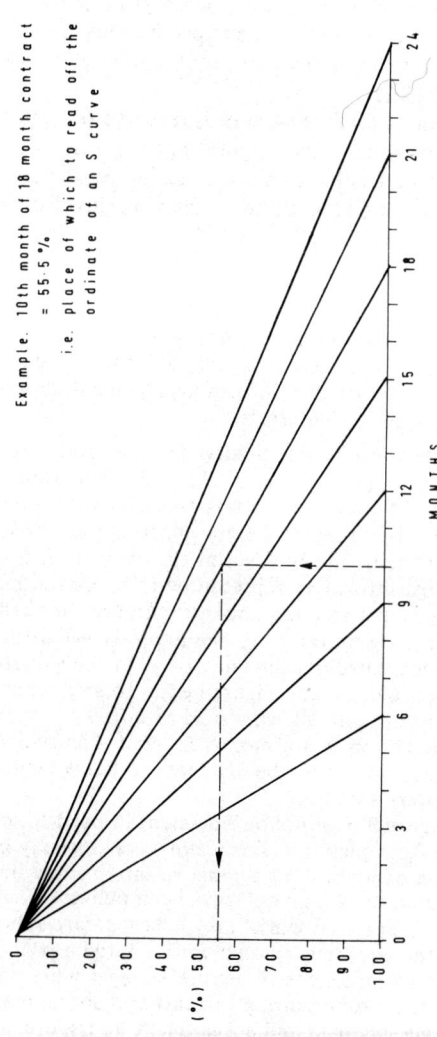

Figure 3.3   Chart for conversion from months elapsed to percentage duration

Forecasting Income

Given an S-curve representing forecast cumulative value, whether of simple geometrical or empirical origin, the value of the ordinate at the percentage duration
(representing the number of months elapsed) represents income, less retention
(usually 5 per cent), and one month in arrears. The zero-margin S-curve in figure
3.2 can be used, in combination with the conversion chart in figure 3.3. Under
the J.C.T. Standard Form of Contract it is to be expected that half of the
retention is released on physical completion, and thus paid one month later, and
the remainder six months after that.

For more immediate contracts some treatment is required for significant
variations, additions, omissions and claims. An allowance against value might
lead to an income adjustment that failed to allow time for negotiations. On the
other hand cost may well have been committed to the work involved.

EXAMPLE 3.1

Prepare a contract budget for a building project, value £56 000, to be completed in 6 months. There is no cost control system within the company,
and the quantity surveyor is required to inform management about the
progress value situation at monthly intervals.

Figure 3.4 illustrates the approximate S-curve for the project with the
monthly forecast valuations tabulated above. Figure 3.5 illustrates the
accumulation of actual valuations in such a way that an overrun of time is
likely. By tabulating the values in figure 3.6 and plotting the realised profit
the surveyor can illustrate the financial effect of the overrun. It is emphasised, however, that the cost information presented in figure 3.6 may be
many days or weeks delayed as this is dependent upon the time taken for
the accountant to arrive at a figure for cost. The monthly valuation is known
when agreed and can be reconciled within a day or so of the valuation date,
but for the accountant to provide a cost figure he has to analyse all amounts
owing, whether invoiced or not and whether paid or not.

Again the profit margin shown is not money in hand. Figure 3.7 shows, in
fact, what the cash flow position might be expected to be. We will return to
cash flow analysis in chapters 4 and 5.

It might appear that figure 3.5 would be sufficient in itself to give early
warning of any deviation from plan, but this is not so. Work may be delayed
or varied and the valuation of work done against variations may be under
negotiation. Expensive equipment may not have been delivered but can be
installed quickly on arrival. External works may be a separate subcontract
held off by weather and the contractor's own work could be proceeding to
programme. A much more comprehensive picture emerges when such a
chart is read along with others representing forecast and actual man-hours,
progress against programme, planned and actual plant hours, etc. These are
more immediately available than cost data.

The quantity surveyor in our example may, of course, estimate his own
cost figure from a review of invoiced liabilities, payroll records and his
reading of progress as a proportion of the total cost involved. Very often a
statement that there is an underrecovery of profit, backed by the necessary.
figures, has a marked effect, which a trend line on a chart would not have.

Figure 3.6 suggests that unless action is taken to restore the margin it could, by projecting the trend line, indicate a lower profit recovery than planned. Indeed, nil profit appears to be a possibility.

Clearly the reconciliation procedures are of fundamental importance.

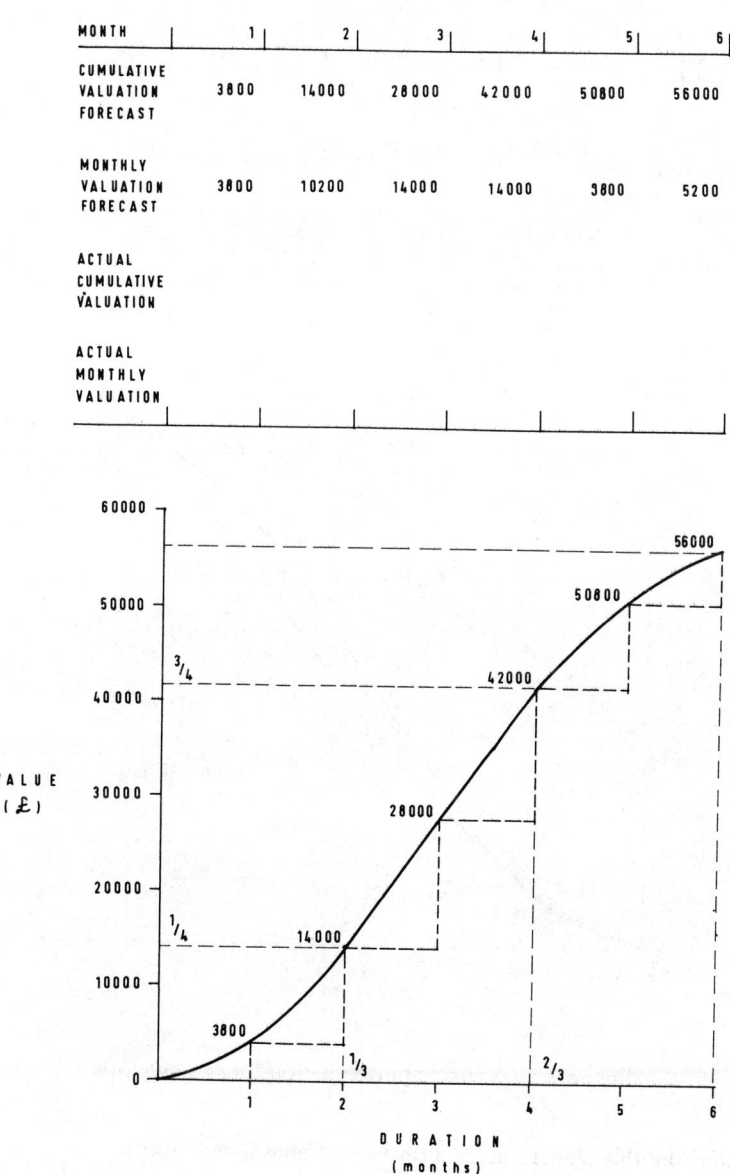

MONTH	1	2	3	4	5	6
CUMULATIVE VALUATION FORECAST	3800	14000	28000	42000	50800	56000
MONTHLY VALUATION FORECAST	3800	10200	14000	14000	3800	5200
ACTUAL CUMULATIVE VALUATION						
ACTUAL MONTHLY VALUATION						

Figure 3.4   S-curve approximation for example 3.1

MONTH	1	2	3	4	5	6
CUMULATIVE VALUATION FORECAST	(3800)	(14000)	(28000)	(42000)	(50800)	(56000)
CUMULATIVE MONTHLY FORECAST	3800	10200	14000	14000	8800	5200
ACTUAL CUMULATIVE VALUATION	5000	15500	26400	39500		
ACTUAL MONTHLY VALUATION	5000	10500	10900	13100		

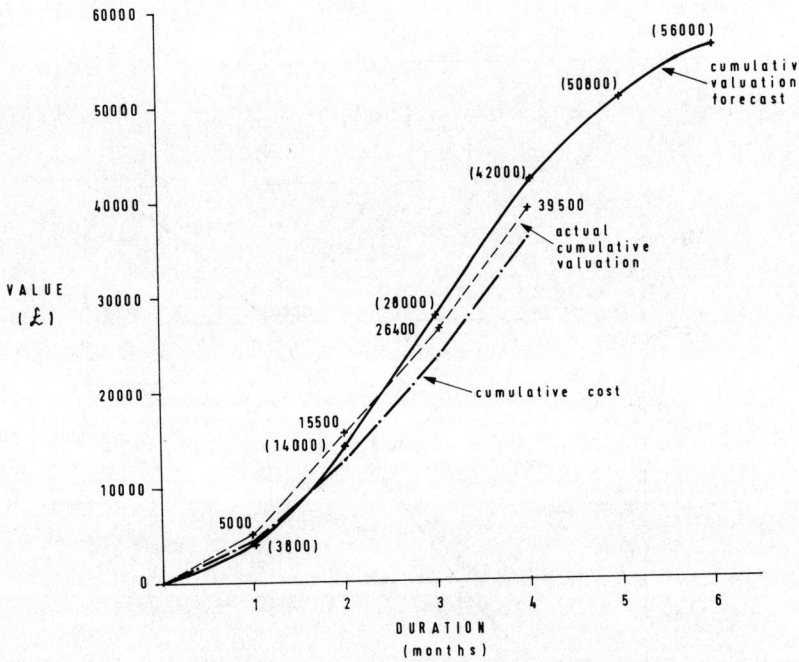

Figure 3.5   S-curve approximation for example 3.1

Adjusting Monthly Valuation Data for Cost –Value Comparisons

In order to enable an accurate cost–value comparison to be made adjustments will have to be carried out in order that the comparisons are valid. The following points will require consideration.

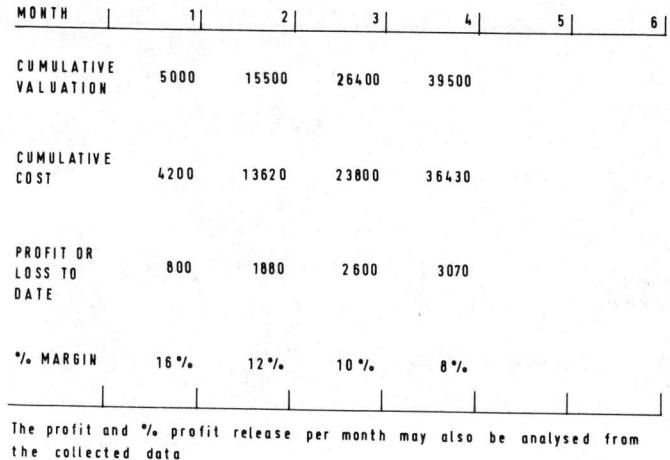

MONTH	1	2	3	4	5	6
CUMULATIVE VALUATION	5000	15500	26400	39500		
CUMULATIVE COST	4200	13620	23800	36430		
PROFIT OR LOSS TO DATE	800	1880	2600	3070		
% MARGIN	16 %	12 %	10 %	8 %		

The profit and % profit release per month may also be analysed from the collected data

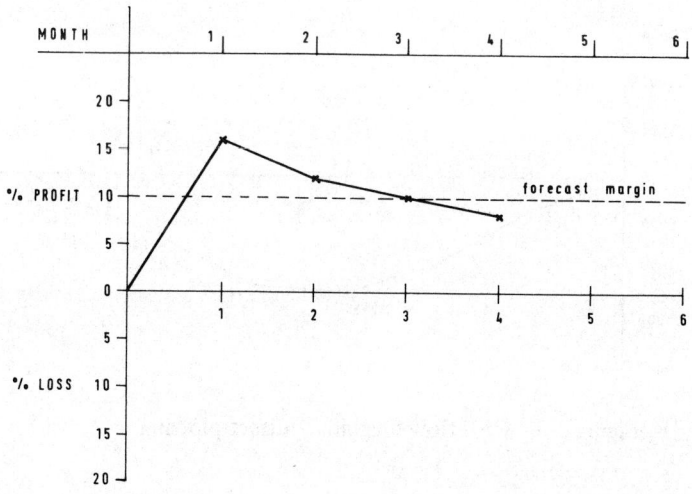

Figure 3.6   Percentage margin release

Cost-Value Reconciliation Dates

Comparison of cost and value should be reconciled to a common date at each month end — say, the 28th day of each month. Where actual valuation dates differ from this, an adjustment in the gross valuation figure, either positive or negative, will be necessary.

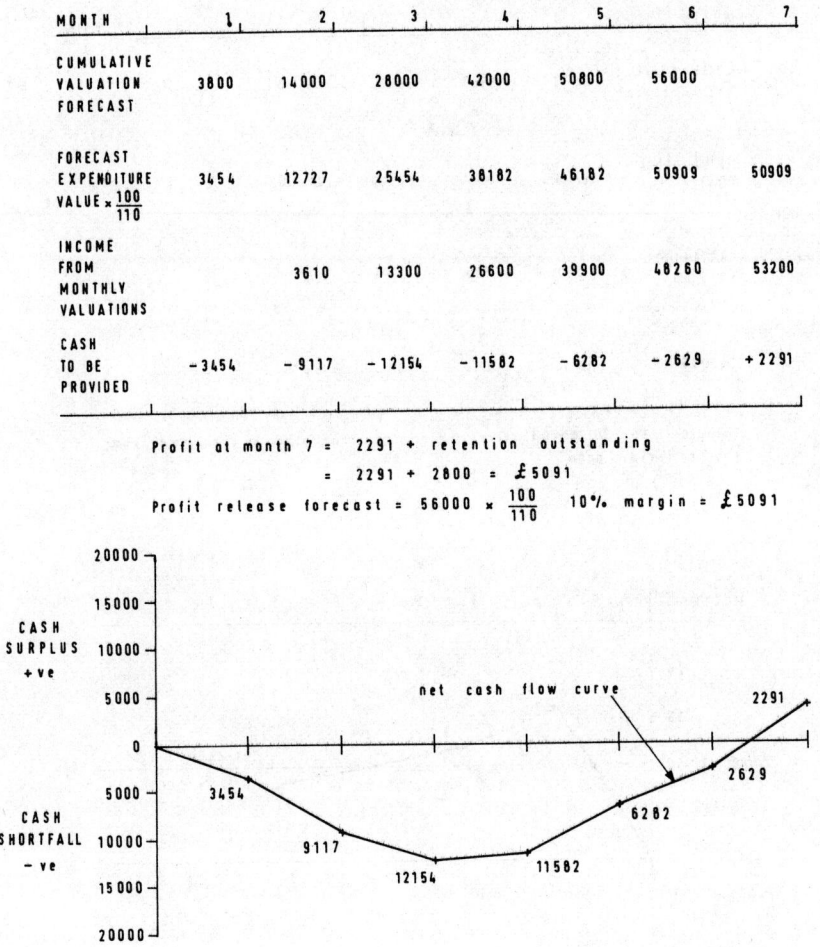

MONTH	1	2	3	4	5	6	7
CUMULATIVE VALUATION FORECAST	3800	14000	28000	42000	50800	56000	
FORECAST EXPENDITURE VALUE $\times \frac{100}{110}$	3454	12727	25454	38182	46182	50909	50909
INCOME FROM MONTHLY VALUATIONS		3610	13300	26600	39900	48260	53200
CASH TO BE PROVIDED	-3454	-9117	-12154	-11582	-6282	-2629	+2291

Profit at month 7 = 2291 + retention outstanding

= 2291 + 2800 = £5091

Profit release forecast = 56000 $\times \frac{100}{110}$ 10% margin = £5091

Figure 3.7　Cash flow diagram – direct plotting

Valuation Adjustments

At the date of the valuation certain items relating to the account may still be unresolved, such as

(1) assessment of claims;
(2) remeasured work sections – submitted but not yet agreed;
(3) variations to contract;
(4) increased costs;
(5) dayworks;
(6) adjustments for materials on site.

In order to provide an accurate assessment of the value of work undertaken, provision will have to be made for any outstanding monies on those items that have
not been included in the valuation — but for which costs have been incurred
against the contract.

The responsibility for internal valuation adjustments normally lies with the
contractor's surveyor in chargeof the project.

The reconciliation may be presented in the form of a surveyor's report or
schedule of adjustments, (see figures 6.1 and 6.2).

EXAMPLE 3.2

Prepare a valuation reconciliation statement at 28 September based on the
following information.

Valuation prepared 5 October; reconciliation date 28 September.

Valuation No. 6 — 5 October 1976:	gross value	£178 300
Valuation No. 5 — 28 August 1976:	gross value	124 200
Gross value for a 5-week period		54 100
Value of work undertaken proportionally per week		10 820
Adjusted valuation to end of September		
Value certified to 5 October 1976		178 300

Deduct

1 week's value proportionately	10 820
Adjusted value to 28 September 1976	£167 480

Add internal adjustments

1 *Variations adjustment*		
Variation order 16–21 assessed value		
5 No. at £150 each	750.00	
2 *Increased costs*		
Labour: week 20–24 (28 September)	800.00	
Material: week 18–24 (approximately)	1 520.00	
3 *Remeasured sections*		
Drainage remeasure — add	1 300.00	
Foundations (soft spots, additional		
hardcore) — add	1 450.00	
4 *Dayworks*		
Daywork sheets 16–20	420.00	6 240.00

Final adjusted value	£173 720.00

Adjustments of valuations may be presented on standard forms or as a monthly
progress return prepared by the job quantity surveyor.

When applying graphical techniques it is important to use adjusted gross value
figures that represent the true contract value position. Only then when the value
is compared with the cost assessment does the financial status of the contract
emerge.

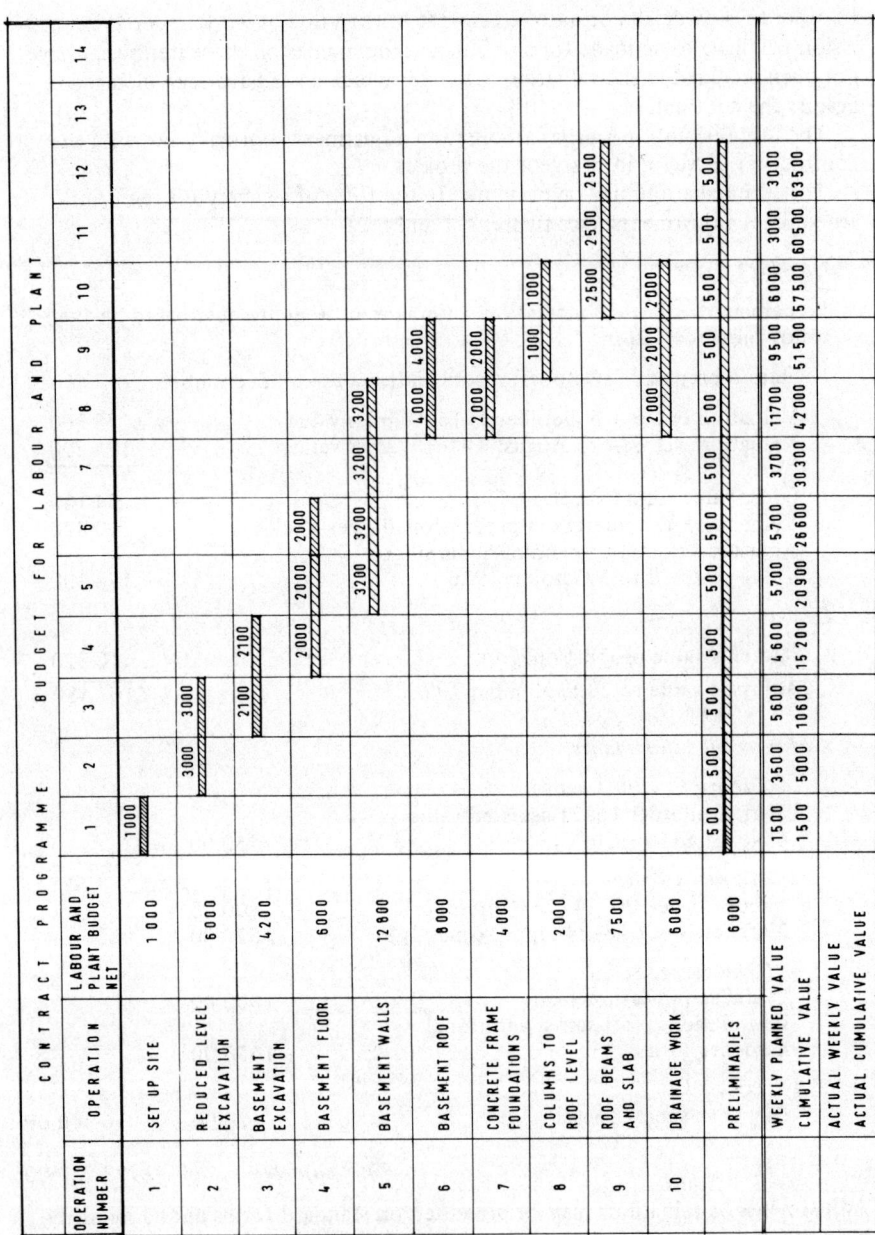

OPERATION NUMBER	OPERATION	LABOUR AND PLANT BUDGET NET	1	2	3	4	5	6	7	8	9	10	11	12	13	14
1	SET UP SITE	1 000	1000													
2	REDUCED LEVEL EXCAVATION	6 000		3000	3000											
3	BASEMENT EXCAVATION	4 200			2100	2100										
4	BASEMENT FLOOR	6 000				2000	2000	2000								
5	BASEMENT WALLS	12 800					3200	3200	3200	3200						
6	BASEMENT ROOF	8 000								4000	4000					
7	CONCRETE FRAME FOUNDATIONS	4 000								2000	2000					
8	COLUMNS TO ROOF LEVEL	2 000									1000	1000				
9	ROOF BEAMS AND SLAB	7 500										2500	2500	2500		
10	DRAINAGE WORK	6 000								2000	2000	2000				
	PRELIMINARIES	6 000	500	500	500	500	500	500	500	500	500	500	500	500		
	WEEKLY PLANNED VALUE		1500	3500	5600	4600	5700	5700	3700	11700	9500	6000	3000	3000		
	CUMULATIVE VALUE		1500	5000	10600	15200	20900	26600	30300	42000	51500	57500	60500	63500		
	ACTUAL WEEKLY VALUE															
	ACTUAL CUMULATIVE VALUE															

CONTRACT PROGRAMME   BUDGET FOR LABOUR AND PLANT

Figure 3.8   Contract budget for labour and plant

Operation Number	Operation	Contract Programme — Labour and Plant Budget Net	Actual Expenditure	1	2	3	4	5	6	7	8	9	10	11	12	13
				Budget for Labour and Plant												
1	SET UP SITE	1000	800	1000 / 800												
2	REDUCED LEVEL EXCAVATION	6000	6400		3000 / 1200	3000 / 2800	/ 2400									
3	BASEMENT EXCAVATION	4200	4000			2100	2100 / 3000	/ 1000								
4	BASEMENT FLOOR	6000	6500				2000	2000 / 2000	2000 / 2500	/ 2000						
5	BASEMENT WALLS	12800						3200	3200 / 2500	3200 / 3900	3200					
6	BASEMENT ROOF	8000									4000	4000				
7	CONCRETE FRAME FOUNDATIONS	4000									4000					
8	COLUMNS TO ROOF LEVEL	2000										1000	1000			
9	ROOF BEAMS AND SLAB	7500										2000	2500	2500	500	
10	DRAINAGE WORK	6000										2000	2000		2000	
	PRELIMINARIES	6000		500 / 400	500 / 450	500 / 450	500 / 500	500 / 450	500 / 400	500 / 450	500	500	500	500	500	
	WEEKLY PLANNED VALUE			1500	3500	5600	4600	5700	5700	3700	11700	9500	6000	3000	3000	
	CUMULATIVE VALUE			1500	5000	10600	15200	20900	26600	30300	42000	51500	57500	60500	63500	
	ACTUAL WEEKLY VALUE			1200	1650	3250	5900	3450	5400	6350						
	CUMULATIVE VALUE			1200	2850	6100	12000	15450	20850	27200						

Figure 3.9   Contract programme — Budget and actual situation

The rapidity with which such statements can follow the date of valuation significantly affects their utility. If control and judgement are to be exercised over the current works, the interval must be in days rather than months.

Contract Budget for Labour, Plant and Preliminaries Control

Budgetary information may be presented directly in the form of a contract programme extended to indicate weekly and cumulative budget values. Figure 3.8 shows a bar chart incorporating forecast budget figures for labour and plant related to each operation to be undertaken. The budgeted figures have been exten-

WEEK NO	1	2	3	4	5	6	7	8	9	10	11	12
PLANNED WEEKLY	1500	3500	5600	4600	5700	5700	3700	11700	9500	6000	3000	3000
ACTUAL WEEKLY	1200	1650	3250	5900	3450	5400	6350					
PLANNED CUMULATIVE	1500	5000	10600	15200	20900	26600	30300	42000	51500	57500	60500	63500
ACTUAL CUMULATIVE	1200	2850	6100	12000	15450	20850	27200					
CUMULATIVE COST	1000	2300	5000	10000	12500	16400						

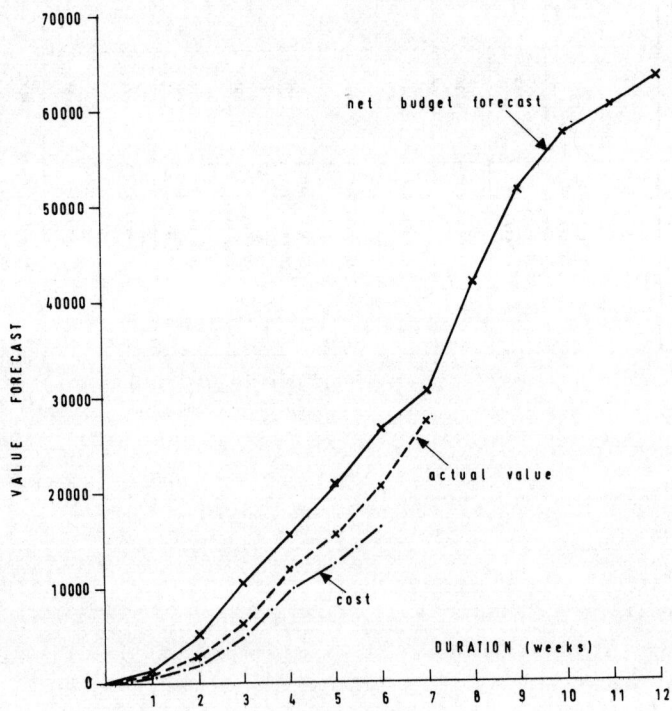

Figure 3.10   Graphical presentation of budget

Item	Plant	Budget	1	2	3	4	5	6	7	8	9	10	11	12	13 (Bud./Act.)	Budg.	Actual cost
1	Crawler tractor 955	450	150/180	150/180	150/180											450	540
2	Hydraulic excavator	1200		200/190	400/470	400/430	200/200									1200	1290
3	Multipurpose excavator	400					200/370	200/400								400	770
4	Dumper	320						40/40	40/40	40	40	40	40	40	40		
5	Tower crane	1800						300/300	300/300	300	300	300	300				
6	Scaffolding	600								100	100	100	100	100	100		
7	B/L mixers	80						10/10	10/10	10	10	10	10	10	10		
8	Fork lift	720								160	160	160	160				
	Forecast weekly budget		150	350	550	400	400	550	350	610	610	610	610	150	150		
	Forecast cumulative budget		150	500	1050	1450	1850	2400	2750	3360	3970	4580	5190	5340	5490		
	Actual weekly expenditure		180	370	650	430	470	750	350								
	Actual cumulative expenditure		180	550	1200	1630	2100	2850	3200								

Figure 3.11 Plant-expenditure budget

ded into weekly and cumulative form to enable comparison with the actual performance achieved on the contract.

Figure 3.9 records the contract position at the end of week 7, showing a comparison of the budget with the actual value released.

Figure 3.10 presents the budget in graphical form. Budget and actual value released may be plotted to show the relationship between the budget and the performance achieved on the contract. As the actual cost situation develops it may be matched with the value released to date.

Figure 3.11 shows a budget prepared for the allocation of plant expenditure. Budgeted monies from the estimate are allocated in a programme format that enables the actual expenditure on plant to be compared with the budget at weekly intervals.

Figure 3.12 is a graphical illustration of the plant budget. At week 7 the budget indicates an overexpenditure of £450. In order to qualify the financial position the progress of the contract must also be assessed. The explanation for

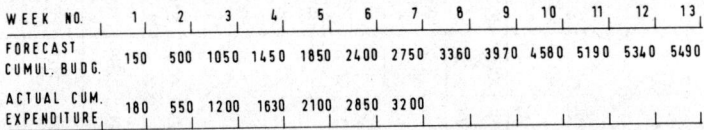

WEEK NO.	1	2	3	4	5	6	7	8	9	10	11	12	13
FORECAST CUMUL. BUDG.	150	500	1050	1450	1850	2400	2750	3360	3970	4580	5190	5340	5490
ACTUAL CUM. EXPENDITURE	180	550	1200	1630	2100	2850	3200						

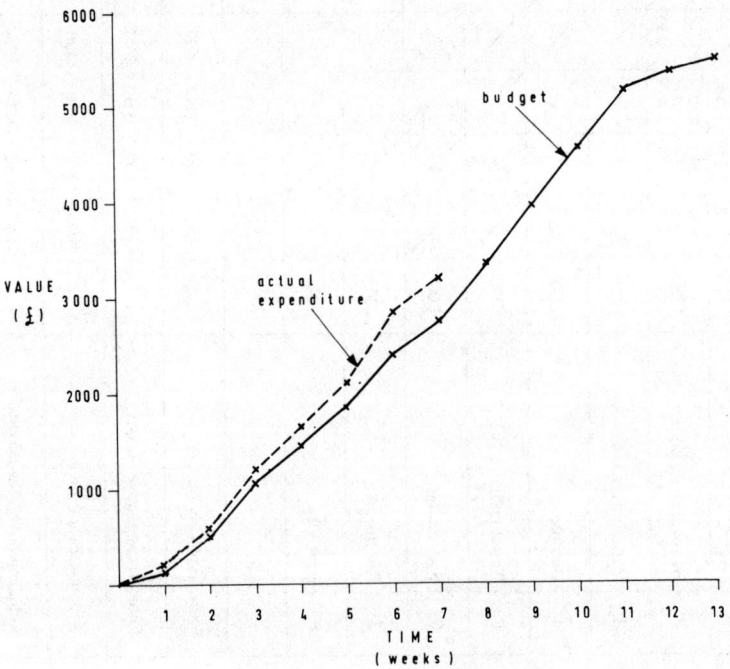

Figure 3.12   Plant budget – graphical presentation

Item	Description/item	Budget/ estimates	1	2	3	4	5	6	7	8	9	10	11	12	13	Budg.	Actual
1	Set up site/fencing	800	400 / 300	400 / 300												800	600
2	Site accomodation	1560	120 / 100	120 / 100	120 / 100	120	120	120	120	120	120	120	120	120	120		
3	Temporary roads	600	300 / 200	300 / 300	— / 50											600	550
4	Site supervision	8020	520 / 400	520 / 400	520 / 400	520	700	700	700	700	700	700	700	520	520		
5	Plant—pumping	320			80	80	80	80									
6	Plant—power crane	1890						270	270	270	270	270	270	270			
7	Plant—scaffolding	1440						180	180	180	180	180	180	180	180		
8	Site transport	240	40 / —	40 / 40	40 / 40	40	40	40									
		14870															
	Forecast weekly budget		1380	1380	760	760	940	1390	1270	1270	1270	1270	1270	1090	820		
	Forecast cumulative budget		1380	2760	3520	4280	5220	6610	7880	9150	10420	11690	12960	14050	14870		
	Actual weekly expenditure		1000	1140	590												
	Cumulative expenditure		1000	2140	2730												

Figure 3.13 Preliminaries budget

the apparent overspending may simply be that the contract is in advance of programme. Analysis of the budget allowance in the estimate compared with the cost indicates overspending on the first three items of plant. The quantity of excavation actually removed should be checked with the bill figures and may result in the submission of a remeasured account for the work. Alternatively the additional costs may have resulted from a change in construction methods or inefficient plant utilisation on site.

Figure 3.13 shows a preliminaries budget of similar format to the plant budget in figure 3.11. The actual expenditure for each preliminary item is built up from weekly site and office returns and indicated in a cumulative weekly form for comparison with the budget as the contract progresses. Overexpenditure on contract preliminaries is a common occurrence on construction projects. In practice some accrue weekly and the number of weeks in the accounting period varies. Only by including actual calender information could a more realistic series of diagrams be produced. As drawn, they relate to a four-week month.

References

Hardy, J. V. *Cash Flow Forecasting for the Construction Industry*, M. Sc. Project (Loughborough University of Technology, 1970).

Nisbet, J., 'Valuations for Interim Certificates', *Architects' Journal* (August 23, 1973).

Singh, Jagjit, *Operations Research* (Penguin, Harmondsworth, 1968).

4 Cash Flow

Cash flow may be defined as the actual movement of money in and out of a business. Money flowing into a business is termed *positive cash flow* (+ve) and is credited as cash received. Monies paid out are termed *negative cash flow* (−ve) and are debited to the business. The difference between the positive and negative cash flows is termed the *net cash flow*.

Within a construction organisation positive cash flow is mainly derived from monies received in the form of monthly payment certificates. Negative cash flow is related to monies expended on a contract in order to pay wages, materials, plant, subcontractors' accounts rendered and overheads expended during the progress of construction operations. On a construction project, the net cash flow will require funding by the contractor when there is a·cash deficit. Where cash is in surplus the contract is self-financing.

The firm itself has other incomes and expenditures. It issues shares and pays dividends, raises loans and pays interests, invests in convertible stocks and sells again when the liquidity of the firm demands it. In effect the term 'funds flow' would be a better term when considering the overall picture.

Operating under U.K. conditions, construction firms undertake their work very largely under contractual terms that maintain them in a state of financial deficit for much of the contract period. Manufacturers of goods are not paid until they sell them but, once a process is established, there is an expectation that sales income will both fund the manufacture of further goods and return a profit. By comparison, the contractor undertakes a relatively small number of discrete but complex operations, being required to finance at any time the difference between the cumulative contractual value of work done, less retention monies, and the cumulative cost of doing the work. The aggregate of a contract's cash flow will then depend on the scale of work and its phasing in with the rest of the firm's work. It follows that there will be periods of deficit and periods of surplus. It is the job of financial managers to raise funds to meet the former and apply surpluses in the best interest of the firm. While we are more concerned with construction management and thus with funds at contract level on individual contracts, we will return to aggregation effects later.

Cash Flow Diagrams

The movement of cash during a contract may be forecast somewhat tentatively from a budget based on an empirical S-curve as illustrated in example 3.1. Alternatively and with more confidence, a forecast of income may be derived

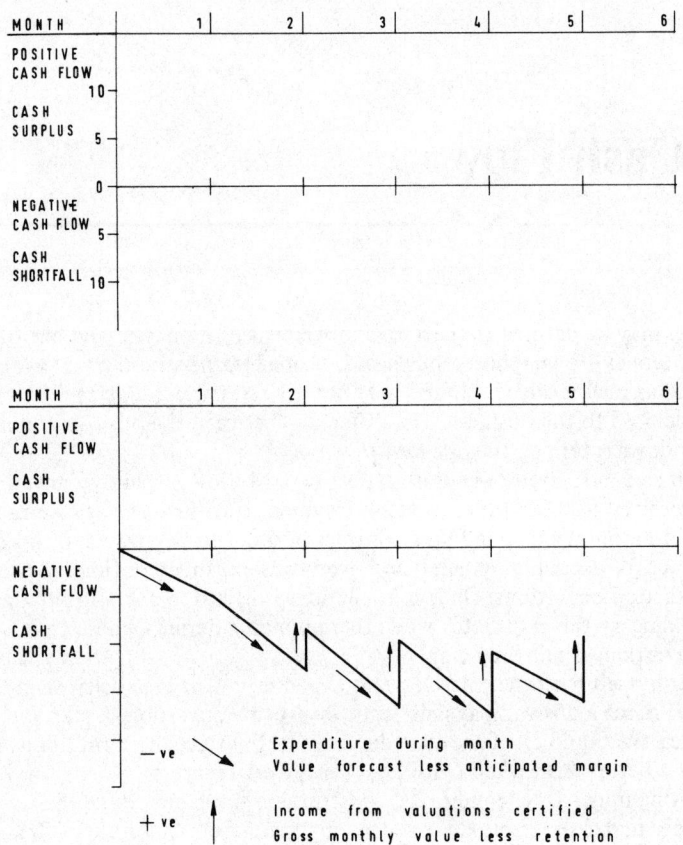

Figure 4.1   Format of cash-flow presentation

from a contract programme prepared at the precontract planning stage. In the examples that follow the income or positive cash flow is assessed from the forecast monthly valuations, adjusted for the retention held. This is plotted vertically on the cash flow diagram in figure 4.1 to represent income received and is released to the contractor one month after the date of the valuation, that is, payment from valuation 1 is received by the contractor at the end of month 2 — if, of course, this is so determined in the contract.

The forecast expenditure or negative cash flow is assessed by assuming that the anticipated profit margin forecast at tender stage will be released proportionately throughout the contract period. This is calculated by deducting the profit release from the forecast valuation and plotting the expenditure proportional to time in the form of a diagonal line on the cash flow diagram. The negative cash flow on the diagram may be referred to as a cash shortfall, and positive cash flow as cash surplus.

The plotting of expenditure (negative cash flow) and income (positive cash flow) in this way results in a sawtooth form of curve, as shown in figure 4.2. The

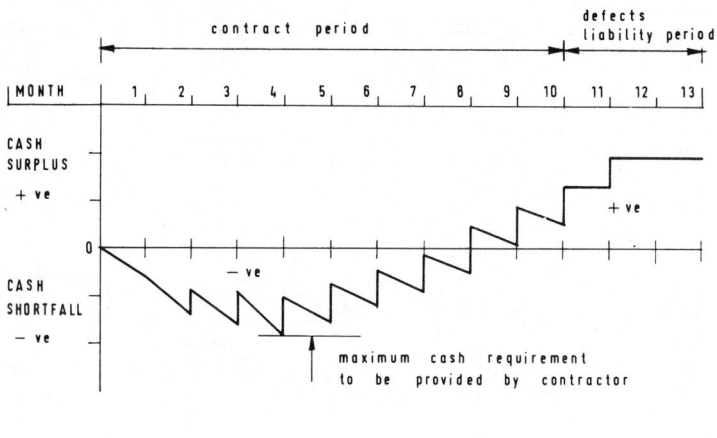

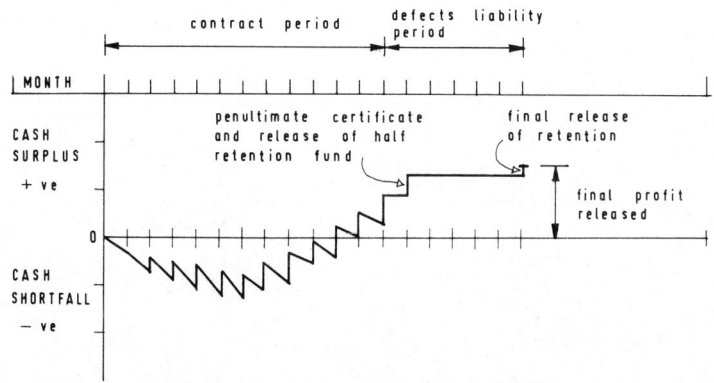

Figure 4.2 Cash-flow presentation – sawtooth diagram

net cash flow may thus be seen as the curve drawn connecting the minumum net cash requirements for the contract, as illustrated in figure 4.3. The maximum net cash requirements may also be shown. The cash flow diagram also indicates the time period during which the contract is self-financing.

In the examples, no account has been taken of the delay in payments due to the contractor's own subcontractors, nominated subcontractors, nominated suppliers and direct material suppliers. Wages for the main subcontractor's own labour will be paid one week after they fall due. Own subcontractors' accounts will be raised monthly and paid 14 days after they become due and similar terms will apply to nominated subcontractors. Nominated suppliers' accounts will be released 30 days after the end of the month during which delivery was made. However, direct material suppliers may be paid on an extended credit basis of one or two months, depending upon the contractor's credit rating with his suppliers. This credit facility can relieve the contractor's cash requirement and

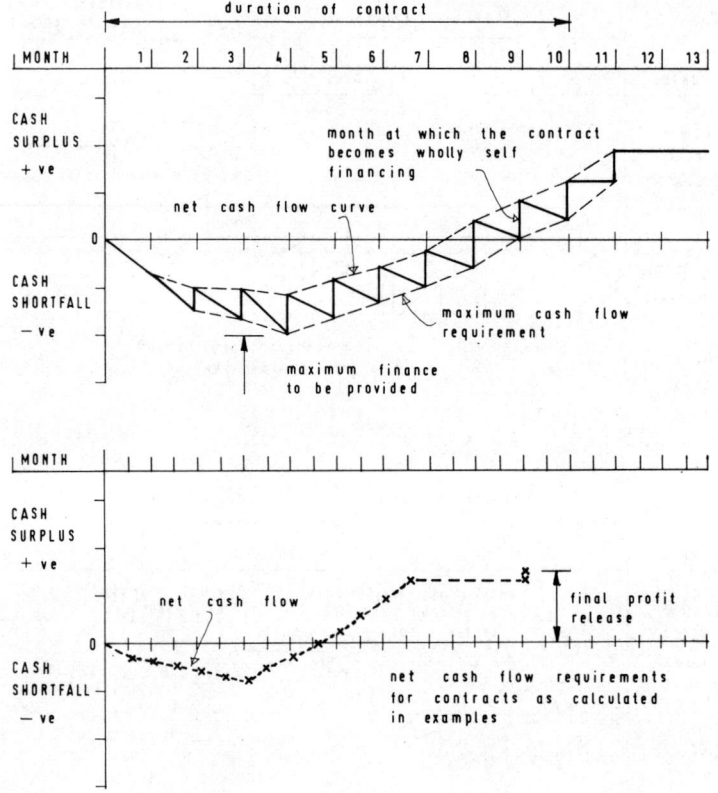

Figure 4.3   Cash flow curves

reduce the cash to be provided by the contractor. Account for delayed payments to material suppliers and subcontractors can be taken into account in cash flow calculations, as in the examples of chapter 5. In practice, a delay of some weeks has come to be expected.

S-curve Presentation of Cash Flow Requirements

By plotting the budget value, forecast cost, and revenue (or income) from valuations against time, one may derive the project cash requirements. The net cash flow can be seen to be the difference between the cumulative contract cost and the income received from valuations at any point in time. Figure 4.4 illustrates the relationship between budget value, estimated cost and revenue. The x ordinate at the beginning of each month represents the net cash flow requirement and the y ordinate at the end of each month gives the maximum cash requirement likely to be made on the contractor.

The calculation of these data may be presented in direct tabular form.

Example 4.1 illustrates the calculation of the cash flow requirements for a contract based on value–time, cost–time and revenue–time relationships.

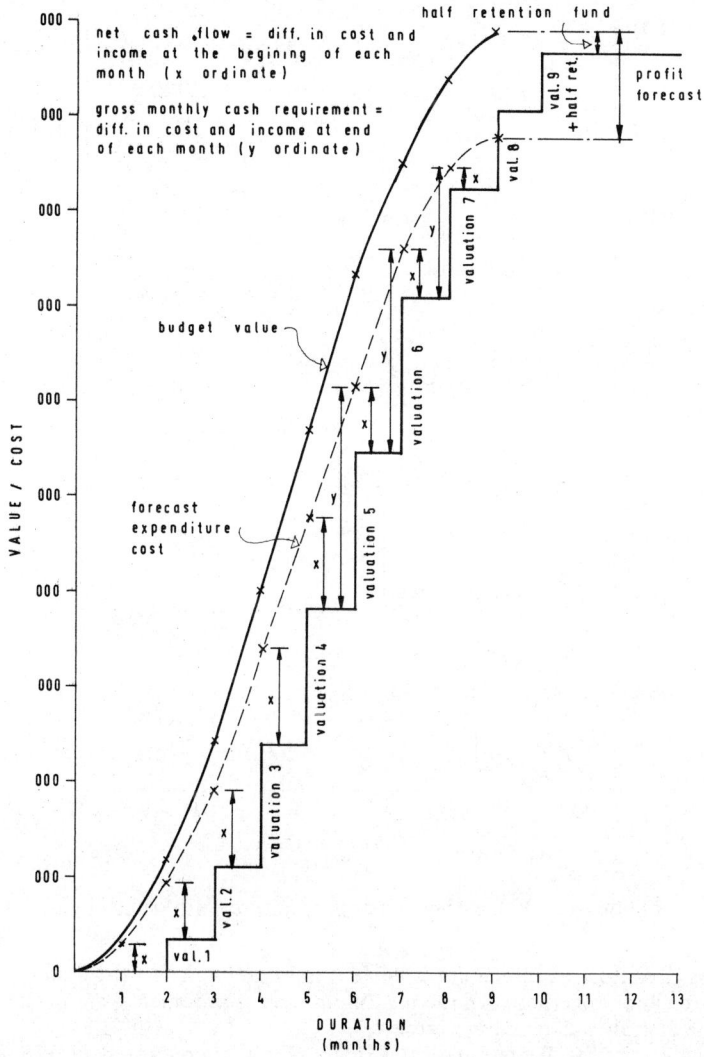

net cash flow = diff. in cost and income at the begining of each month (x ordinate)

gross monthly cash requirement = diff. in cost and income at end of each month (y ordinate)

half retention fund

profit forecast

budget value

forecast expenditure cost

val.1

val.2

valuation 3

valuation 4

valuation 5

valuation 6

valuation 7

val. 8

val. 9 +half ret.

VALUE / COST

DURATION
(months)

Figure 4.4 Presentation of cash flow on S-curve

EXAMPLE 4.1

Calculate the cash-flow requirements to be provided by a contractor under-taking a contract valued at £80 000 and of 9 months' duration. The cash requirements are to be based on a forecast profit release of 20 per cent. Retention money of 5% is to be held during the contract, the figure being reduced to $2\frac{1}{2}$ per cent at contract completion. The defects-liability period is 6 months.

Figure 4.5 gives the value–time, cost–time and revenue–time curves based

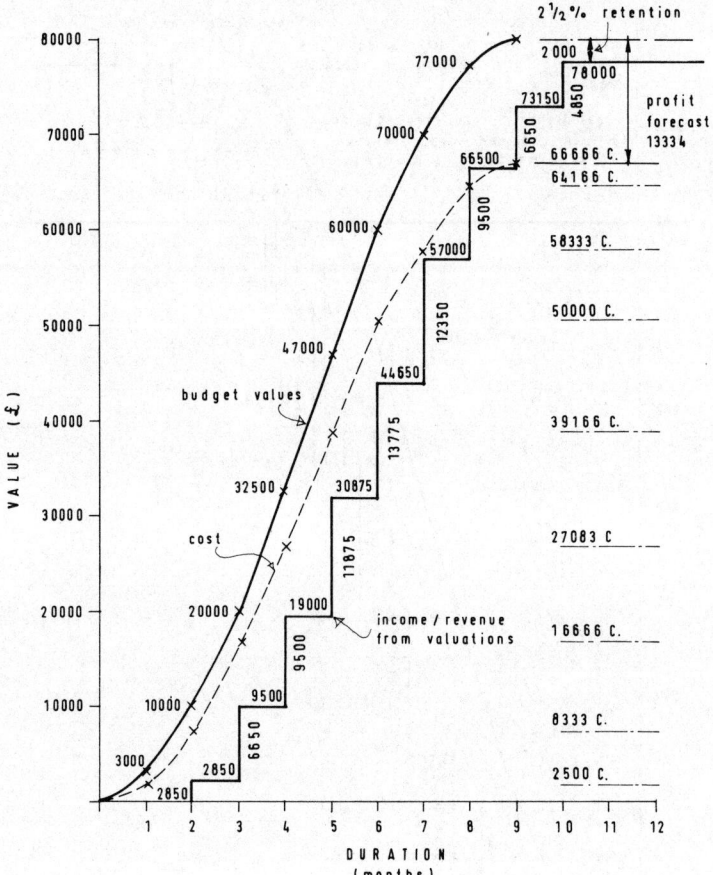

Figure 4.5   Value–time, cost–time and revenue–time curves

on the cash flow requirements calculated in Figure 4.6. The net cash flow requirements, together with the maximum cash requirements, are presented on the cash flow diagram in Figure 4.7.

Analysis of the diagram indicates that a maximum requirement of £20 166 is to be provided at the end of month 5. At month 8 and 9 the contract becomes partially self-financing and may then become wholly self-financing at month 10, at the release of the final payment to the contractor.

EXAMPLE 4.2

Calculate the cash flow requirements to be provided by the contractor undertaking a contract valued at £100 000 and of 9 months' duration. All work is to be undertaken by the main contractor.

Retention money of 5 per cent is to be held during the contract, the figure being reduced to $2\frac{1}{2}$ per cent at contract completion. The defects-liability period is 6 months. Assume that a 20% margin will be realised.

Month	Date	A Monthly budget	B Cumulative budget	B – profit ×100/120 Cost or contract expenditure	B – 5% ret. Money received (cumulative -retention)	–ve shortfall Net cash flow	A – 5% ret. Net monthly income	Gross Max. cash requirement
1		3000	3000	2500	–	–2500	–	–2500
2		7000	10000	8333	2850	–5483	2850	–8333
3		10000	20000	16666	9500	–7166	6650	–13816
4		12500	32500	27083	19000	–8083	9500	–17583
5		14500	47000	39166	30875	–8291	11875	–20166
6		13000	60000	50000	44650	–5350	13775	–19125
7		10000	70000	58333	57000	–1333	12350	–13683
8		7000	77000	64166	66500	+2334	9500	–7166
9		3000	80000	66666	73150	+6484	6650	–166
10		–			76000 + 2000 ret. 78000 2000 ret. 80000	+11334 +13334	2850 + 2000 ret. 4850	

Figure 4.6   Cash flow assessment – tabular presentation

MONTH	1	2	3	4	5	6	7	8	9	10
NET CASH	− 2500	− 5483	− 7166	− 8083	− 8291	− 5350	− 1333	+ 2334	+ 6484	+ 11334
	− 2500	− 8333	− 13816	− 17583	− 20166	− 19125	− 13683	− 7166	− 166	

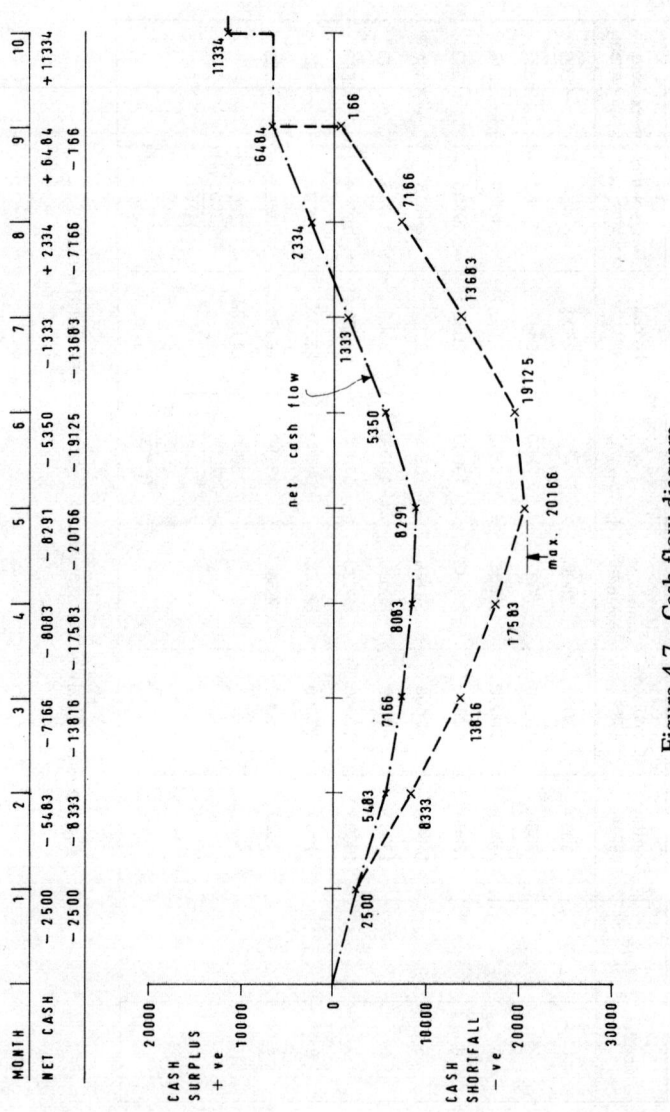

Figure 4.7 Cash flow diagram

Budget value of work to be undertaken

The values may be abstracted from the approximate S-curve for the project based on the 1/4–1/3 approximation (see figure 4.8).

Valuation No	Gross value forecast (cumulative)	Monthly forecast valuation
1	4000	4000
2	12 000	8 000
3	25 000	13 000
4	41 000	16 000
5	57 000	16 000
6	75 000	18 000
7	87 000	12 000
8	96 000	9000
9	100 000	4000

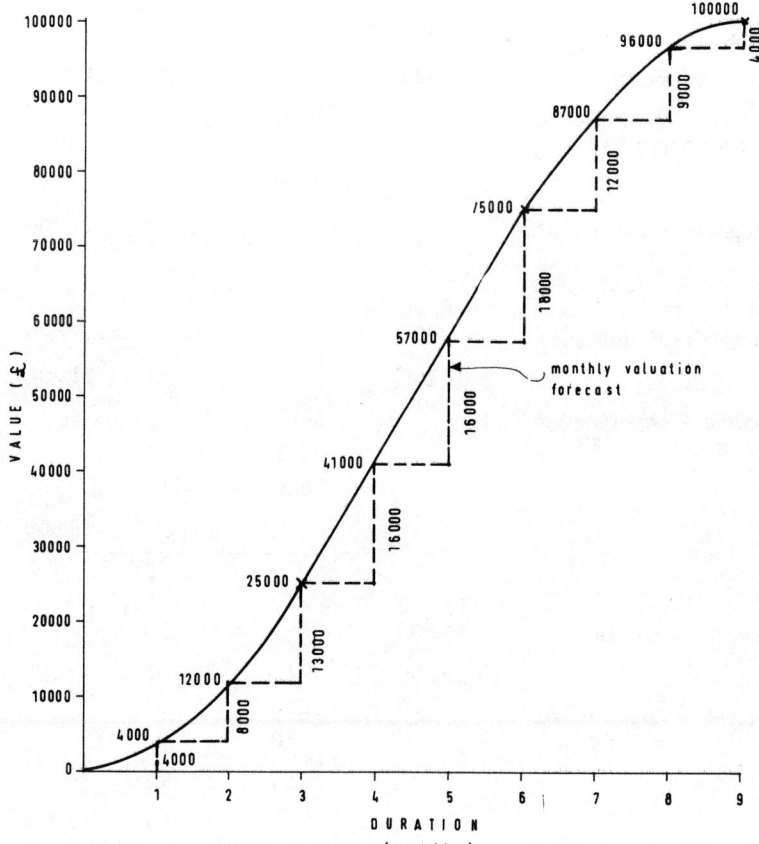

Figure 4.8 Forecast valuations from S-curve

Adopt the conservative assumption that monthly budget represents cost*. If a profit margin is assumed then the value of cash deficits will be reduced and the forecast of finance required likewise less than it would otherwise be. As we are dealing with forecasts over a long term, which will be periodically updated, such prudence is often the best course.

The cash flow calculation has been developed from basic principles indicating the cash flow requirements excluding profit and then adjusted for the profit release.

Assessment of Cash Requirements Monthly

(No allowance has been made for the profit adjustment.)

Month 1

Budget for month	4000			
Income during month	—			
	4000			4000

Month 2

Budget for month	8000			
To end of month 2	12 000		12 000	12 000
Income – valuation No. 1		4000		
Less retention 5%		200		
		3800	3800	
Budget to end of month			8200	8 200

Month 3

	8200			
Budget for month	13 000			
	21 200		21 200	21 200
Income – valuation No. 2		8000		
Less Retention 5%		400		
		7600	7600	
			13 600	13 600

Month 4

	13 600			
Budget for month	16 000			
	29 600		29 600	29 600
Income – valuation No. 3		13 000		
Less Retention 5%		650		
		12 350	12 350	
			17 250	17 250

*i.e. no profit will be realised.

Month 5	17 250			
Budget for month	16 000			
	33 250		33 250	33 250
Income – valuation No. 4		16 000		
Less retention 5%		800		
		15 200	15 200	
			18 050	18 050
Month 6	18 050			
Budget for month	18 000			
	36 050		36 050	36 050
Income – valuation No. 5		16 000		
Less retention 5%		800		
		15 200	15 200	
			20 850	20 850
Month 7	20 850			
Budget for month	12 000			
	32 850		32 850	32 850
Income – valuation No. 6		18 000		
Less retention 5%		900		
		17 100	17 100	
			15 750	15 750
Month 8	15 750			
Budget for month	9000			
	24 750		24 750	24 750
Income – valuation No. 7		12 000		
Less retention 5%		600		
		11 400	11 400	
			13 350	13 350
Month 9	13 350			
Budget for month	4000			
	17 350		17 350	17 350
Income – valuation No. 8		9000		
Less retention 5%		450		
		8550	8550	
			8800	8800

Month 10
(penultimate account)   8800
  Budget for month   –

                                8800   8800   8800

    Income – valuation No. 9   4000
    Less retention 5%   200

                                     3800   3800
                                                   5000   5000

Release of $2\frac{1}{2}\%$ 5000
Retention at penultimate
  account   2500

                                      2500
Release of final retention
 ·at end of defects
  liability period   2500

                     £   –

The gross budgeted cash requirements assessed at the beginning and end of each month have been plotted in figure 4.9 to represent the cash requirement including the profit margin.

Adjustment for Profit Release

If we assume that net cost is less than the monthly budget then we can provide for the release of profit. If in our example we provide for a margin of 20% of the net value of work undertaken, then the calculations are adjusted as follows

$$£100\,000 \times \frac{100}{120}$$

  = $100\,000 \times 0.833$ = 83 333 net contract value
Add profit margin 20%   16 667 total contract profit

                £100 000

The profit release on the monthly budget forecast will therefore be as follows.

Month 1
  Budget £4 000
  × 0.833   3 333 Contractor's net cost

        £ 667 Contractor's profit released at month 1

Profit release figures for each month are shown in tabular form and on the cash flow requirements curve in figure 4.10. These figures indicate that the contract might attain a cash surplus at the beginning of month 9 of £2682 and a cash shortfall at the end of month 9 of £683.
    Consider the release of the remaining payments at the end of contract.

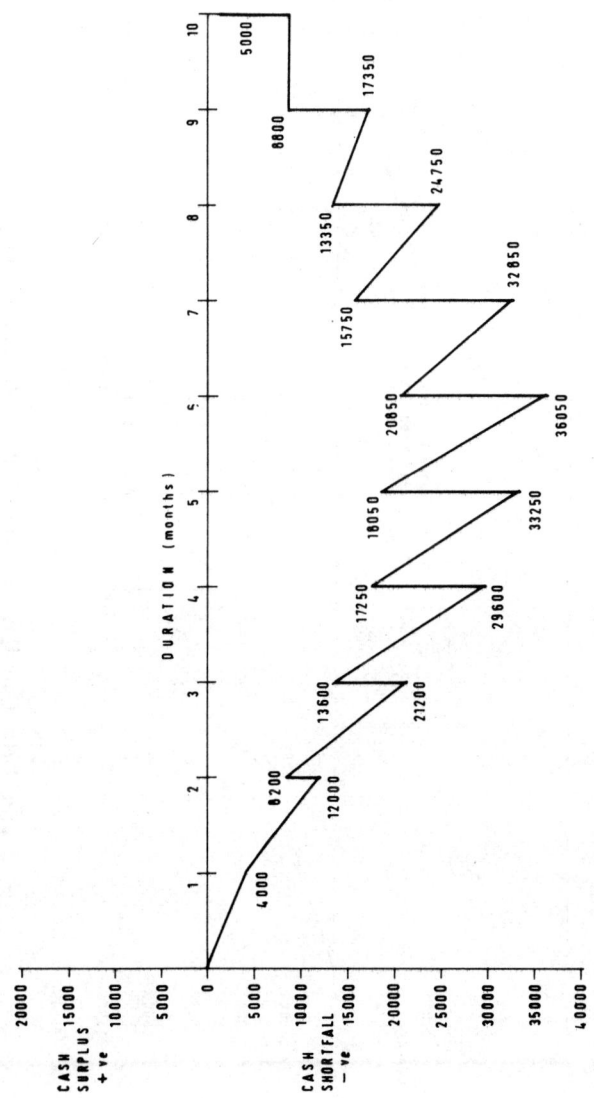

Figure 4.9 Cash flow diagram – no allowance for profit adjustment

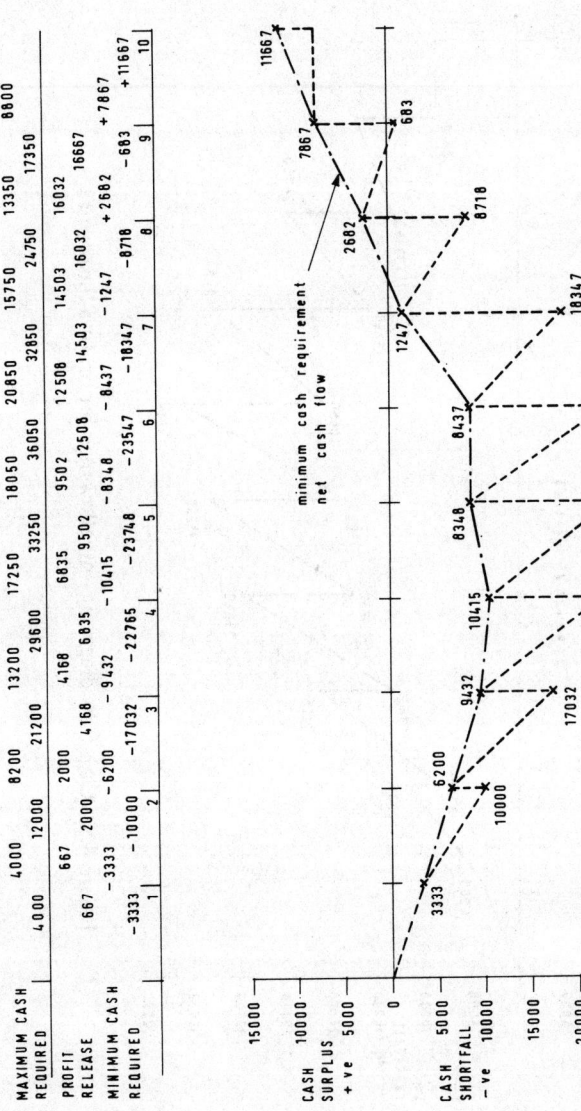

MAXIMUM CASH REQUIRED	4000	4000	8200	13200	17250	18050	20850	15750	24750	13350	8800
PROFIT RELEASE		667	2000	4168	6035	9502	12508	14503	16032	16667	
	667	2000	4168	6035	9502	12508	14503	16032	17350		
		2000	29600	33250	36050	32850	14503	16032	+2682	+7867	+11667
MINIMUM CASH REQUIRED		−3333	−6200	−9432	−10415	−8348	−8437	−1247	−8718	−683	
	−3333	−10000	−17032	−22765	−23547	−10347					
	1	2	3	4	5	6	7	8	9	10	

Figure 4.10   Cash flow diagram — with profit adjustment

Cash shortfall at the end of the contract   −683

Monies due at month 9 − valuation No. 8	+8 550	
Monies due at month 10 − valuation No. 9	+3 800	
Retention released at month 9 − valuation	+2 500	
Retention released at end of maintenance period	+2 500	
	+17 350	−683
	−683	
Contractor's profit	£16 667	

Minimum and Maximum Net Cash Requirements

Calculation of the minimum and maximum net cash requirements indicates that the contract becomes self-financing and shows a cash surplus of £2682 at the beginning of month 9, the final profit of £16 667 being achieved on release of the outstanding retentions.

Net Cash Flow

Month	Minimum cash requirements	Maximum cash requirements
1	−3 333	−3 333
2	−6 200	−10 000
3	−9 432	−17 032
4	−10 415	−22 765
5	−8 548	−23 748
6	−8 347	−23 547
7	−1 247	−18 347
8	+2 682	−8 718
9	+7 867	−683

This summarises the minimum and maximum cash to be provided by the contractor throughout the contract period.

Direct Presentation of Minimum Net Cash Flow

This may be presented in direct tabular form (table 4.1) and plotted in the form of a net flow curve.

Maximum net cash requirements may be assessed by adding the net valuations received to the net cash requirements.

The minimum and maximum cash requirements are plotted in figure 4.11, and assimilate the sawtooth presentation from figure 4.10.

Financial Requirements to Fund Cash Flow

The finance to support a forecast deficit after clearing accounts due at the end of each month must be raised on a long-term basis, whereas the interim payments may be covered on a short-term basis.

A line connecting the points on the cash flow curve nearest the axis thus indicates the demand for long-term finance. The sum of such demands over the duration of the firm's contract represents the deficit against which to set retentions and debtors to produce a working profit. Where the firm's overdraft limit exceeds that strictly necessary to fund the monthly expenditure (because it is a

Table 4.1   Cash Flow Calculation Tabular Presentation

Month	Monthly Budget A	Cumulative Budget B	Contract Expenditure —Cost B-profit release	Money rec. to Date —ve Retention B-retention	Net Cash Required —ve shortfall +ve surplus	Net Monthly Income A-retention	Max. Cash Req.	Notes	
1	4 000	4 000	3 333	—	-3 333	—	-3 333	Min. cash req. during contract	£683
2	8 000	12 000	10 000	3 800	-6 200	+3 800	-10 000	Max. cash req. during contract	£23 748
3	13 000	25 000	20 832	11 400	-9 432	+7 600	-17 032		
4	16 000	41 000	34 165	23 750	-10 415	+12 350	-22 765	Contract profit	20% 16 667
5	16 000	57 000	47 498	38 950	-8 548	+15 200	-23 748		
6	18 000	75 000	62 497	54 150	-8 347	+15 200	-23 547		
7	12 000	87 000	72 497	71 250	-1 247	+17 100	-18 347		
8	9 000	96 000	79 968	82 650	+2 682	+11 400	-8 718		
9	4 000	10 000	83 333	91 200	+7 867	+8 550	-683		
			Monies released month 10	3 800	+11 667				
			Retention released month 10	2 500	+14 167				
			Final release of retention	2 500	+16 667				

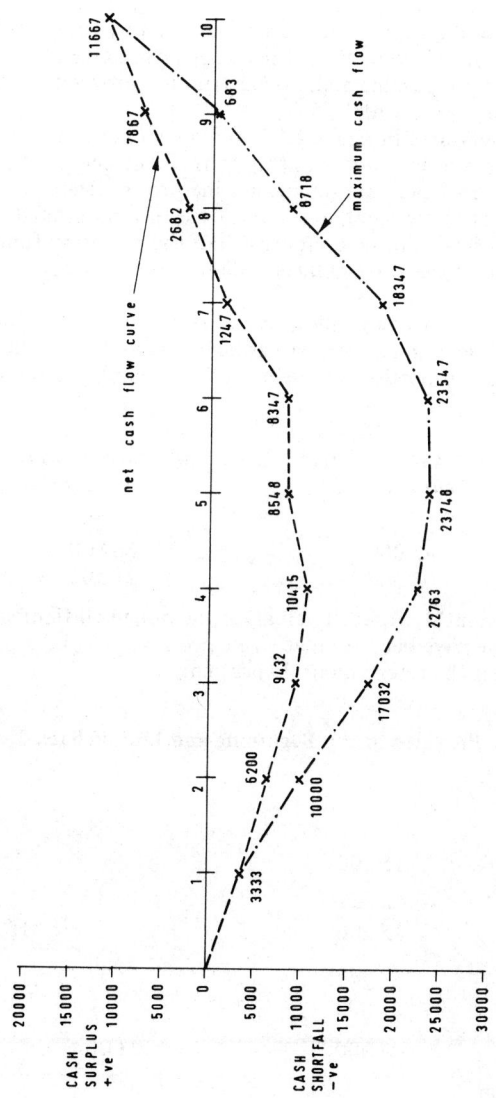

Figure 4.11 Cash flow diagram – net and maximum cash-flow requirements

less expensive source of finance than those otherwise available) a line through
the points on the cash'flow curve furthest from the axis indicates the maximum
demand for finance. From the maximum cash demand, subtracting the overdraft
limit, we arrive at a figure for the essential long-term finance to be provided.

EXAMPLE 4.3

Budget forecasts that depend on the S-curve are superseded by forecasts based
on more precise information. At some time it becomes possible to base the
forecast on a construction programme and, as construction proceeds, on short-
term programmes and progress records.

From the contract programme in figure 4.12, prepare a cash flow analysis
for the contract. Payment is to be made monthly to the contractor within a
period of 28 days, subject to 2 per cent retention. The profit release from the
project has been forecast at 10 per cent. The contract is of 3 months' duration
and the defects-liability period is to be 6 months. Half the retention fund is to
be released on completion of the work and the balance on completion of the
defects period.

Figure 4.13 shows the forecast value plotted against the contract duration
to assimilate an S-curve. The cumulative cost has been assessed by assuming
that the release of profit is proportional to value and time, and this has also
been indicated.

Valuation No.	Gross value forecast (cumulative)	Monthly forecast valuation
1 (week 4)	15 200	15 200
2 (week 8)	42 000	26 800
3 (week 12)	63 500	21 500

In order to arrive at the monthly forecast valuation the budgeted figures per
week from the programme have been totalled. Valuation No. 1 will be paid
at the end of month 2, less the retention of $2\frac{1}{2}$ per cent.

Assessment of Cash to be Provided at the Beginning and End of Each Month

Monthly Cash Requirements

Month 1

Budget for month	15 200			
Income during month	—			
	15 200			15 200

Month 2

Budget for month	15 200			
	26 800			
To end of month	42 000		42 000	
Income from valuation				
No. 1		15 200		
Less retention $2\frac{1}{2}\%$		380		
		14 820	14 820	
			27 180	27 180

OPERATION NUMBER	OPERATION		CONTRACT PROGRAMME													
			JANUARY				FEBRUARY				MARCH					
			1	2	3	4	5	6	7	8	9	10	11	12	13	14
1	SET UP SITE	1000	1000													
2	REDUCED LEVEL EXCAVATION	6000		3000	3000											
3	BASEMENT EXCAVATION	4200			2100	2100										
4	BASEMENT FLOOR	6000				2000	2000	2000								
5	BASEMENT WALLS	12800					3200	3200	3200	3200						
6	BASEMENT ROOF	8000								4000	4000					
7	CONSTRUCT FRAME FOUNDATIONS	4000								2000	2000					
8	COLUMNS TO ROOF	2000									1000	1000				
9	ROOF BEAMS AND SLAB	7500										2500	2500	2500		
10	DRAINAGE WORK	6000								2000	2000	2000				
	PRELIMINARIES	6000	500	500	500	500	500	500	500	500	500	500	500	500		
	WEEKLY PLANNED VALUE		1500	3500	5600	4600	5700	5700	3700	11700	9500	6000	3000	3000		
	CUMULATIVE VALUE		1500	5000	10600	15200	20900	26600	30300	42000	51500	57500	60500	63500		

Figure 4.12 Contract programme – budget

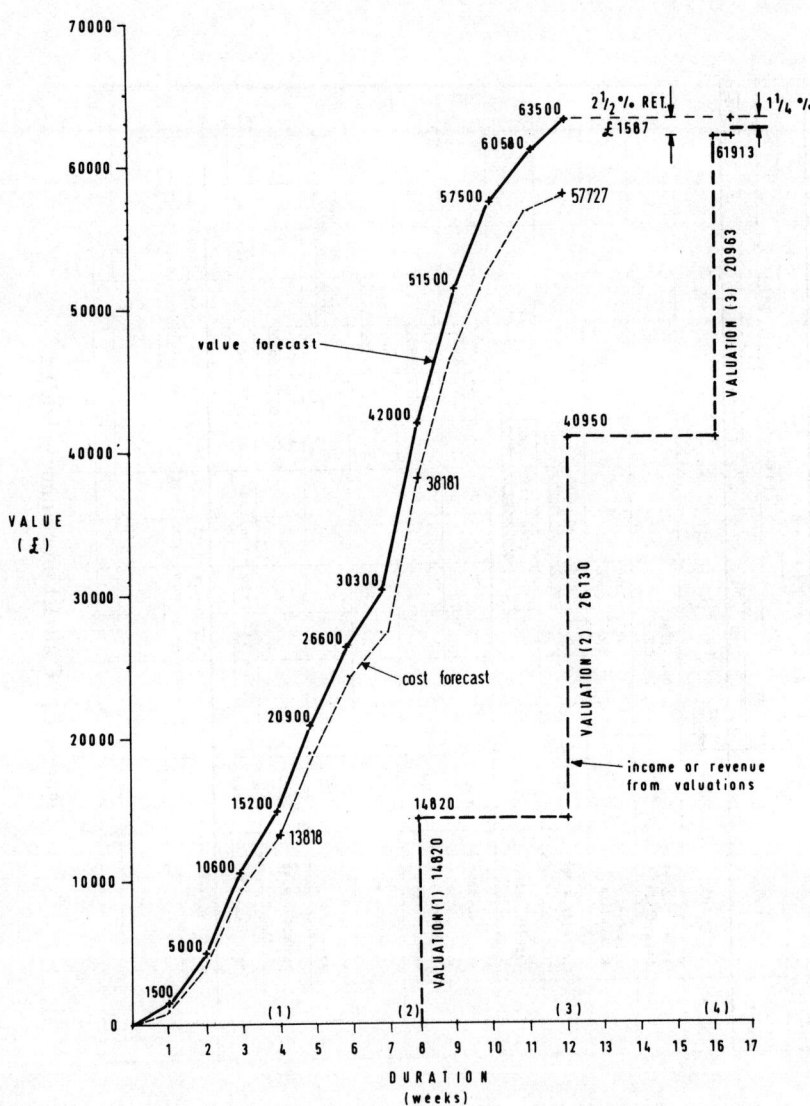

Figure 4.13   Value–time, cost–time and revenue–time curves

Month 3	27 180			
Budget for month	25 100			
To end of month	48 680		48 680	
Income from valuation No. 2		26 800		
Less retention $2\frac{1}{2}\%$		670		
		26 130	26 130	
			22 550	22 550
Month 4	22 550			
Budget for month	—			
To end of month	22 550		22 550	
Income from valuation No. 3		21 500		
Less retention $2\frac{1}{2}$		537		
		20 963	20 963	
			1587	1587

Release of Retention

Release of $1\frac{1}{4}\%$ retention at penultimate account	794
Valuation No. 3 $1\frac{1}{4}\% \times 63\,500$	
	793
Final release of retention at end of maintenance period	
Month 9 $1\frac{1}{4}\% \times 63\,500$	793
	—

The gross budgeted cash requirement assessed at the beginning and end of each month is presented in figure 4.14 to represent the cash requirement to be provided, including a profit margin of 10%.

Adjustment for Profit Release

A profit release of 10% has been assumed throughout the contract, that is

$$63500 \times \frac{100}{110} = \text{£}57\,727$$

Add margin of 10% =	5773
	£63 500

The profit release on the monthly budget forecast will therefore be as follows.

Month	1	2	3	4	5
Budget forecast (A)	15 200	42 000	48 680	22 550	1587 ($2\frac{1}{2}\%$ retention to be released)
	15 200	15 200	27 180	22 550	1587
Cumulative budget value (B)	15 200	42 000	63 500	—	
Profit release/expenditure $C = B \times \frac{100}{110}$	13 818	38 181	57 727	57 727	
Profit release to date (D)	1382	3819	5773	5773	
Net cash required (E = A − D)	−13 818	−38 151	−42 907	−16 777	$\dfrac{4186}{1587}$ + ret. = 5773 release profit; +4186
	−13 818	−13 818	−23 361	−16 777	
Minimum net cash (F)	−13 818	−13 818	−23 361	−16 777	
Maximum net cash (G)	−13 818	−38 181	−42 907	+4186	

Figure 4.14   Cash flow assessment — tabular presentation

Month 1

Budget 15 200

$$\text{Contractor's net cost} = \frac{100}{110} \times 15\,200 = 13\,818$$

Profit release month 1 £1382

Profit release figures for each month are indicated in tabular form in figure 4.14 and graphically in figure 4.15.

This indicates that the contract attains a cash surplus at the end of month 4.

Cash surplus at month 4 £4186

To this must be added the 1¼% retention released at this date amounting to:

$1\frac{1}{4}\% \times £63\,500$ £793

A further retention release will also fall due at the end of the defects-liability period of a similar amount £793

Total profit release from contract £5772

This is equivalent to the contractor's anticipated profit from the contract

10% of £57 727 = £5 772

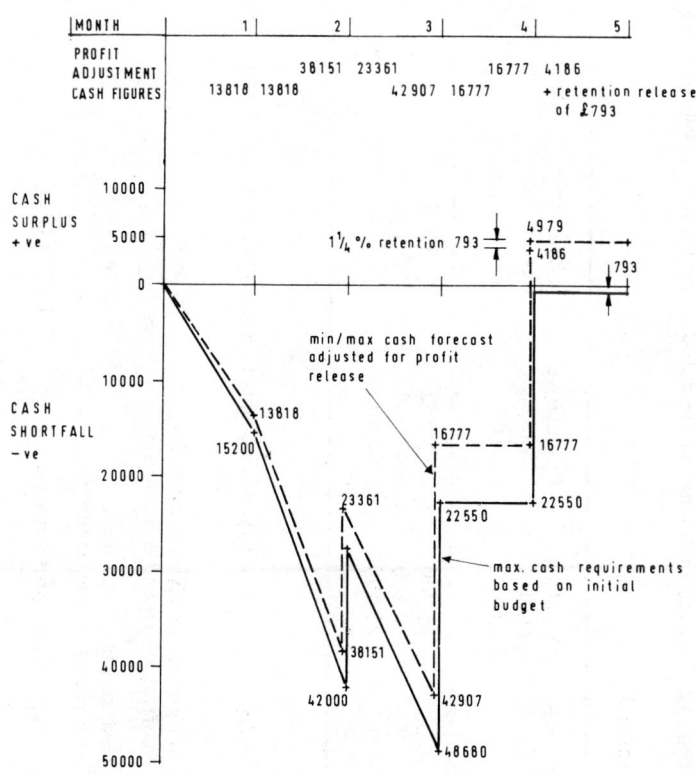

Figure 4.15 Sawtooth diagram with and without profit adjustment

Direct Presentation of Minimum Net Cash Flow

The cash-flow requirements are presented in the form of a cash-flow curve in figure 4.16, and are also given in table 4.1.

Table 4.2

Month	Monthly budget (A)	Cumulative budget (B)	Contract expenditure (B - profit)	Monies received to date less retention (B - $2\frac{1}{2}$% ret.)	Minimum cash required*	Net monthly income (A - $2\frac{1}{2}$%)	Maximum cash required
1	15 200	15 200	13 818	–	–13 818	–	–13 818
2	26 800	42 000	38 181	14 820	–23 361	14 820	–38 181
3	21 500	63 500	57 727	40 950	–16 777	26 130	–42 907
4	–	–	–	61 913			

*A negative quantity corresponds to a shortfall, and a positive quantity to a surplus.

Net monies received at month 4	20 953
Shortfall up to end of month 3	–16 777
Cash surplus at month 4	4 186
Add retention outstanding	1 587
Total profit release	£5 773

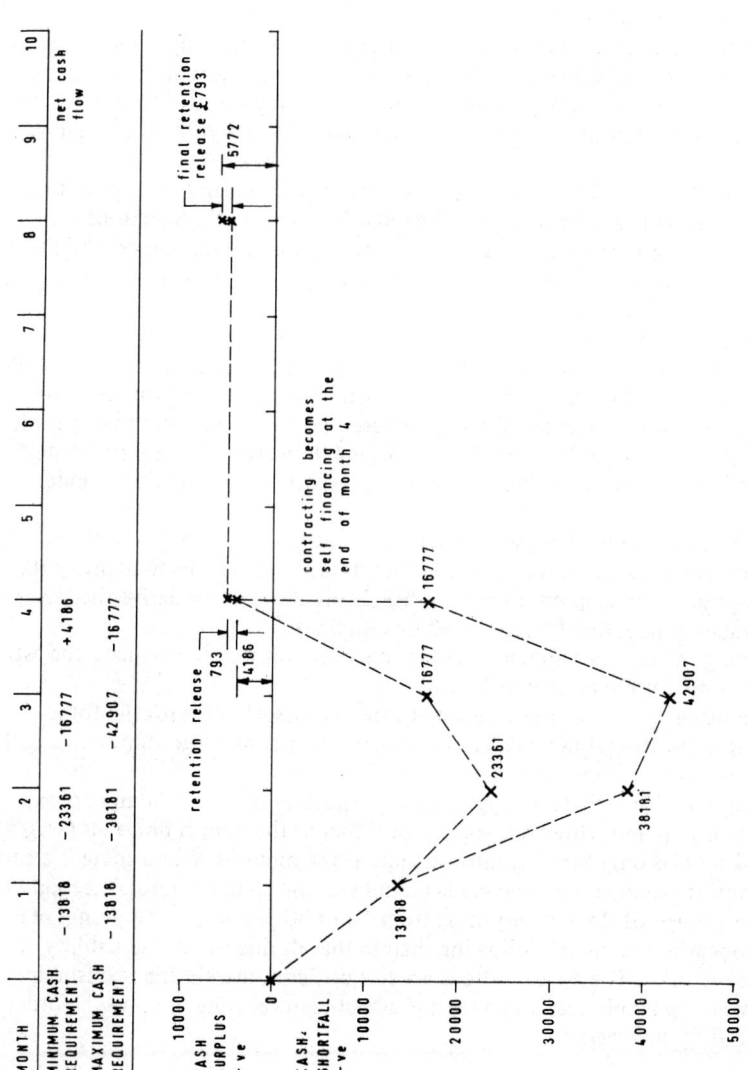

Figure 4.16 Direct plotting of cash flow requirements

Cash Flow Aggregations for Budgeting

In any calender month there will be a variety of sizes and types of contract each at a different stage of completion. Each contract will either be in cash deficit or surplus, and the cash-flow situation of the firm will be represented by the algebraic sum of these amounts.

From figures estimated in respect of materials to be called up, subcontractor progress, plant hire and so on, each site quantity surveyor can project cost for future months. From a review of valuations it is equally possible to predict the month's income corresponding to estimated cost. The difference is the net cash-flow forecast.

For one or two months ahead such estimates allow demand for liquid funds to be forecast with some assurance. Site quantity surveyors' projections are summed, additions are made for headquarters' income and outgoings, and the accountant seeks favourable terms for financial support or advice on the best use to be made of any surplus.

Beyond a few months the task of prediction is less easy. Contracts may be identified by contract sum and duration and a proposed starting date only. Contriving a cash-flow forecast on the basis of S-curve data at least provides some indication of financial trends. Simulation based on past experience may permit a probabilistic model to be used directly. Where, however, a geometric model is to be used, the assumptions incorporated are important and should be understood.

Any calendar month represents a stage of contract duration. From figure 3.3, the month concerned and the total contract duration permit us to identify the percentage duration elapsed. From figure 3.2 this allows us to derive the percentage cumulative valuation (using the nil-margin line).

Knowing the contract sum and deducting retention we can calculate the estimated income *for the month following.*

Again using figure 3.2, but referring to the line associated with the forecast margin, interpolating if necessary, we can arrive at a percentage cumulative cost (again based on the contract sum).

The probability is that, for aggregation purposes, this is as near an approximation as is required. However, some cost is met as the month proceeds (wages, etc.) and some is only brought into account at the month end and there is a further month before payment need be made (suppliers' and subcontractors' accounts). At various stages of the job, anything from 10 to 80 per cent of outgoings may better appear in the month following than in that during which the liability is estimated to arise. The computations are not difficult, merely time-consuming, and may very possibly result in a trifling adjustment, bearing in mind the order of uncertainty involved.

EXAMPLE 4.4

The following contracts were listed and a starting date was allocated by use of random numbers so that the outcome would be unpredictable.

Contract (A)   £211 100 in 18 months returning 10% starting $M - 12$
Contract (B)   £79 720 in 12 months returning 15% starting $M - 4$
Contract (C)   £56 400 in 6 months returning 15% starting $M - 3$

Contract (D)	£89 720 in	9 months returning 15% starting $M + 4$
Contract (E)	£281 300 in	24 months returning 10% starting $M + 8$
Contract (F)	£15 580 in	6 months returning 15% starting $M + 11$

The budget is to be for 12 months from month M.

In practice the income and expenditure for $M-1$ would be known. In the example we calculate it using the S-curve model.

The tabulated outcome gives

(1a) contract month;
(1b) percentage duration;
(1c) percentage valuation;
(1d) percentage cost based on estimator margin;
(2a) cumulative income based on one-month delay, 10% retention, half of which is repaid with the final interim certificate (on physical completion) and the remainder at the end of the defects-liability period;
(2b) cumulative cost;
(2c) monthly projected cash flow.

The calculations for any one month are as follows.
Take any month, say, month 3 ($= M + 2$), for, say, contract A.

Contract A started in $M - 12$.

The month selected is then the 15th month of the contract. The receipt during the 15th month will, however, be that of the valuation at the 14th month less retention (in this case 10%) or 0.9 of the amount of the valuation.

From figure 3.3 (p. 27) the ordinate at 14 months cuts the 18-month contract duration line at 77%. From figure 3.2 (p. 26) this corresponds to a percentage completion of 86% and thus the income will be

$$0.86 \times 211\,100 \times 0.9 = 163\,391$$

From figure 3.3 the ordinate at 15 months cuts the 18-month contract duration line at 83%. The cost is determined by the intersection of the 83% completion ordinate on the curve in figure 3.2 corresponding to a 10% margin, that is, 82% of the value

$$0.82 \times 211\,100 \qquad = \underline{173\,102}$$

the finance required $= \underline{\quad 9\,711}$

After the final month (that is, at the forecast time of physical completion) there remain

(a) the uncollected increment of value earned in the last month (less retention) — payable the following month;
(b) the released retention (usually half) due on physical completion — payable the following month;
(c) the retention released at the end of the defects-liability period (usually due six months after physical completion and paid the following month).

In the case of contract C for instance

(a) £56 400 less 10% less the £46 699 previously due
  = £50 760 − 46 699)   = £4 061
(b) £56 400 × 0.05   = £2 820   £6 881

(c) £56 400 × 0.05   £2 820

Budget month

Contract		M − 1	M (1)	2	3	4	5	6	7	8	9
A	a contract month	12	13	14	15	16	17	18	(19)		
	b % duration	66	72	77	83	88	94	100	*		(13)
	c % valuation	75	81	86	91	94	97	100			
	d % cost	–	73	77	82	86	88	90			*
B	a contract month	4	5	6	7	8	9	10	11	12	(13)
	b % duration	33	42	50	59	67	75	83	92	100	*
	c % valuation	25	38	50	63	75	84	91	96	100	
	d % cost	–	32	43	54	64	72	78	82	85	
C	a contract month	3	4	5	6	(7)					(12)
	b % duration	50	67	84	100	*					*
	c % valuation	50	75	92	100						
	d % cost	–	64	78	85						
D	a contract month					*	1	2	3	4	5
	b % duration						11	22	33	44	56
	c % valuation						4	12	26	43	57
	d % cost						3	10	21	36	50
E	a contract month									*	1
	b % duration										4
	c % valuation										1.5
	d % cost										1
F											

* Repayment of retention monies due

Figure 4.17 Budget aggregation (S-curve estimates)

Contract		M-1	M (1)	2	3	4	5	6	7	8	9
								Budget month			
A*	a cumulative value	127293	143 493	153 892	163 391	172 891	178 591	184 290	(189 990)		
	b cumulative cost		154 103	162 547	173 102	1811 546	185 768	189 990			
	c balance		−11 610	−8655	9711	−8655	−7177	−5700	+16 255	+	
B	a	10 762	17 937	27 264	35 874	45 201	53 811	60 268	65 291	68 870	71 748
	b		25 510	34 280	43 049	51 021	57 398	62 182	65 370	67 762	
	c		−7573	−7024	−7175	−4820	−3587	−1914	−89	+1116	+6845
C	a	12 690	25 380	38 070	46 699	(50 760)					
	b		36 096	43 992	47 940						
	c		−10 716	−5922	−1241	+6881	+				
D							−	3220	9690	20 994	34 721
							2692	8972	18 841	32 299	44 860
							−2692	−7742	−9151	−11 305	−10 149
E											−
											2813
											−2813
F											
Positive cash flow									7820		
Negative cash flow			29 899	26 395	18 127	6594	13 456	12 549		10 996	5191

Figure 4.18 Budget aggregation and net cash flow requirements

   Thus to sustain a volume of work running at £280 878 p.a. or £23 407 per month the firm requires finance that varies from just under £30 000 in any one month to nil. The average is £12 659. Figures 4.17 and 4.18 indicate the budget aggregation in tabular form.

5 The Effect of Delayed Payments on the Contractor's Cash Requirements

Improving the Cash Flow

It will have become clear that the balance of cash at any time represents effort expended not only in production but in gaining and making payment, and indeed also in gaining an appropriate sequence of work. There are aspects of site performance that can be seen to aid the general cash-flow position, or harm it, but managing the financial performance of a firm demands a capacity to overview activities for which few managers receive any help or training. Thus many senior managers are happier in demonstrating their grasp of site-production matters than in acquiring and utilising a command of management techniques relating to the control of broader aspects of their firm's affairs. As Brown (1970) has remarked; 'daily routine drives out planning', and it is tempting to do what is familiar and available, and to put aside other things.

Those at different levels of responsibility may form different assessments of the benefit to be derived from an action. The site quantity surveyor may see advantages in delaying proceedings in connection with a claim. There may be a number of minor unresolved issues. Coping with an overcautious architect or private quantity surveyor is often easier and less likely to result in a harsh settlement if matters are handled a lot at a time rather than singly. There is personal glory in rectifying an apparently adverse situation in the process of negotiating the final certificate. However, when the firm's working capital is but a small part of its annual turnover[1] —as one would expect in construction—then the rate at which it is turned over is crucial to the return gained by the firm on the capital. For capital turned over eight times a year, as Robertson (1977) has pointed out, a $2\frac{1}{2}$ per cent profit on turnover would produce a 20 per cent return. If, however, because of slow payments, undervaluations, hidden retentions, release of retentions not made, certificates not paid and the like the capital turnover falls to four times then the return would drop to 10 per cent.

Reynolds and Hesketh (1973) record an average of 3.6 as the number of times capital employed was turned over per annum in 1970.

It must be admitted that doing the work correctly and expeditiously is the first and basic step towards being paid. Quite clearly, however, there are failures to understand and apply the letter and spirit of the conditions of contract and

---

[1] In fact Reynolds and Hesketh (1973) found working capital to be much the same proportion of capital employed as for other industries, although 'stock and work in progress' were a greater part of it. Capital employed in 1970 averaged 34.5 per cent of turnover.

these can introduce delays in payment.

We have mentioned the decision to hold back for more propitious times the processing of claims by the contractor. The main contractor can raise cash flow problems for subcontractors by withholding payment until he is paid, by reluctance to forgo his $2\frac{1}{2}$ per cent discount even when he fails to pay within 14 days, and by dilatory treatment of fluctuations or small matters which may thus delay the settlement of a final account. The subcontractor may of course fail to produce essential documents and create the delay himself.

Apart from delay in settling claims, the contractor may prolong the settlement of variation work rates and the agreement of accounts. He may be concentrating on the next job and neglect items of making good and small matters that await checking in aid of settlement, so as to delay the final account.

The quantity surveyor may be more concerned with future work and so make no moves to progress other matters in his office. He can fail to value variations during the currency of the work, and delay giving the architect information on which to base his interim certificate. By excessive caution in avoiding overpaying, he may introduce a margin of hidden retention.

In turn, the architect may impress his own overcaution on the process. He may extend the processing of the certificate beyond the permitted seven days after valuation and, in particular, delay certificates of practical completion or even partial practical completion that might release funds to which the contractor is entitled. He may fail to press on the employer his responsibility to facilitate the payment of amounts covered by his certificates (and employers also have cash flow problems).

It can be seen that the spirit of contract conditions can easily be lost if observance is allowed to depart from the letter, and all concerned must recognise that if they seek to bend rules to their convenience then others will assuredly do likewise.

The insidious thing about cash shortage is that, under a system of measurement and payment that imposes negative cash flow for much of a contract, a deficit can very easily creep past the point of no return, unless the contractor's managers are vigilant. If cash and near-cash is unable to sustain a sudden request for payment, even though by liquidation the firm might demonstrate its solvency, then trading may cease. Managers should be uneasy in a situation of continuing cash shortage. Such unease should prompt a number of lines of enquiry. Parsons (1976) has suggested that delay in producing company accounts beyond three or four months from the accounting date should give rise to such anxiety. If a delay is explicable, doubts should be allayed by a preliminary statement. Creditors may otherwise become uneasy, press for payment and precipitate a crisis. A firm that can produce a cash flow forecast, backed by financial-control procedures and evidence of a realistic marketing-based budget exercise has more chance—in fact every chance— of satisfying its bank and other creditors and being bridged over a temporary cash deficit.

It is very rarely in the employer's interest to have on his hands a contract that has to be determined because of the financial embarrassment of his contractor. The situation has been discussed elsewhere. If then, by ensuring that all responsibilities are observed under the contract, the employer and his advisers do their part, it is up to the senior managers of a contracting company to extend control, in a detailed sense, from production through administrative controls to budgeting and marketing policy and thus to anticipate the demand and supply of essential resources to meet their part of the contract.

Cash Flow—Payment of Accounts

The cash flow situation as indicated in the worked examples assumes that the cost commitment for payment to subcontractors and suppliers is raised in the month in which the work is undertaken.

Payments for labour employed by the contractor will be paid one week after they fall due. Domestic subcontractors' and nominated subcontractors' accounts should be raised monthly and paid 14 days after certification. Nominated suppliers' accounts fall due 30 days from the end of the month during which delivery was made. Direct material suppliers' accounts may however be paid within 30 days to qualify for cash discount or on an extended-credit basis, depending upon the credit rating of the contractor; extended credit has attractions in times of high interest rates. Suppliers' accounts may therefore fall due for payment one or more months after the end of the month in which delivery is made. Suppliers themselves are not punctilious in the presentation of accounts and, when still qualifying for cash discount, a proportion of such accounts will be three or more months' old.

It is clear then that the assumption of the model errs on the side of prudence. It assumes that liabilities will be met promptly, and thus that the finance required in the early stages of a contract will be more than experience leads us to expect. If there has to be a margin then it is of the right sort, since it leaves something for contingencies.

The S-curve is at best an empirical model representing a firm's past experience of a particular form of work, and at its worst a geometrical approximation. If, therefore, a firm has data by which to construct an empirical S-curve it should also be able to derive its typical cash-flow curve. This would include the effect of the firm's accounting policies on cash flow. Research by Hardy (1970) suggests that projects of the same type had similar forms of S-curve goemetry when value and time were expressed in percentage format. Therefore any device to allow for delays in payment by means of an amended geometrical S-curve procedure is an approximation of an approximation and, in terms of liquidity, to sail so near the wind is to court disaster. Of those who practise S-curve budgeting there are few who consider any such refinement. The view is that the S-curve approximation refers to future work, and immediate forecasts (next and succeeding month) are almost wholly based upon the current statements of account of live contracts and the progress forecasts of site staff. At three months and beyond, forecasts are extremely speculative. However, policy alternatives as well as forecasts may gain by the procedures outlined below.

It should also be noted that the effect is most marked in the cash-flow forecast of an individual contract. Budgets are summations of the cash flows of many contracts. The effect of monthly forecasts of cash outflow and inflow will be moderated by summation. Marketing action rather than credit manipulation would be the direct response to a forecast of an excessive future cash deficit.

Figure 5.1 shows the contractor's commitment for payment of account during

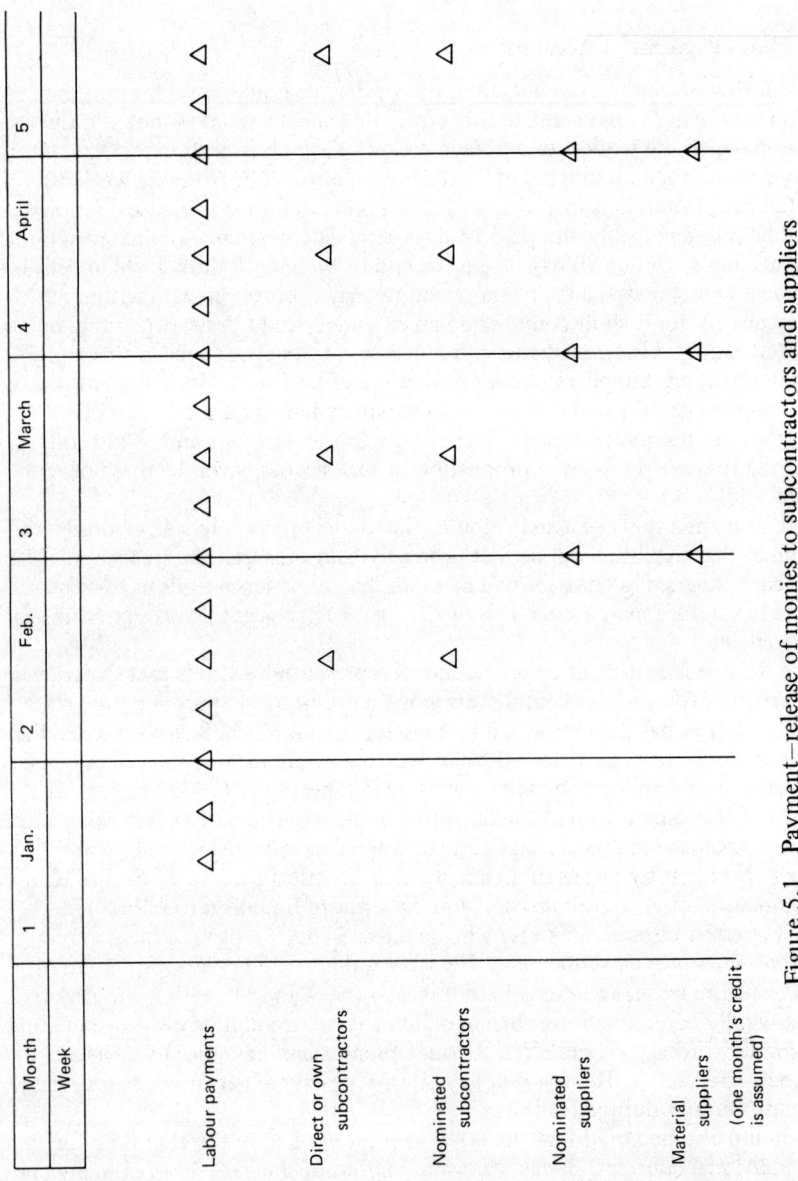

Figure 5.1   Payment—release of monies to subcontractors and suppliers

the normal progress of a single contract. The effect of delayed payments to sub-contractors and suppliers will normally be to improve the contractor's cash-flow postition and reduce his cash requirements *for the contract,* which may or may not be desirable from the viewpoint of the firm as a whole.

Research into cash flow forecasting at Loughborough University by McKay (1971) and Kerr (1973) has produced analytical techniques based on manual and computer analysis. McCaffer (1975) indicates the use of a simplification using weighted-average payment delays, applied to cost headings. This weighted-average delay applied to the total cost gives 'cash out' figures, which are relatively accurate over the duration of a contract except during the first few weeks and the last few weeks.

By introducing adjustments to the production factors of labour, plant, materials and subcontractors to the various stages of work in progress, one can assess a weighted-average delay for payments at any stage. This involves assessing the percentage of the cost attributed to each cost heading by analysis of the contribution distribution throughout the project. This information is obtained from the estimating department. The cumulative cost–time figures can then be produced in percentage terms.

Weighted-average Delay

The procedure is to calculate the weighted-average payment delay for all cost headings, the weighting being the percentage of cost due to that heading. We might assume, for example, that during the contract the cost distribution is as in table 5.1.

Table 5.1

Cost heading	Weighting (%)	Payment delay (weeks)
Labour	30	1.0
Material	40	4.0
Plant	10	4.0
Subcontractor	20	2.0

The weighted-average delay in this case is as follows.

Labour	$30\% \times 1.0 = 0.30$
Material	$40\% \times 4.0 = 1.60$
Plant	$10\% \times 4.0 = 0.40$
Subcontractor	$20\% \times 2.0 = \underline{0.40}$
	2.90

Let us say, then, that the weighted-average delay is 3 weeks.

The total cost commitment at the end of each month will be delayed by 3 weeks. By approximation, monies due at the end of month 1 (week 4) will be released at the end of week 7. A similar delay in the release of monies will also occur at the end of each succeeding month.

The effect of the weighted-average delay is shown diagrammically in figures

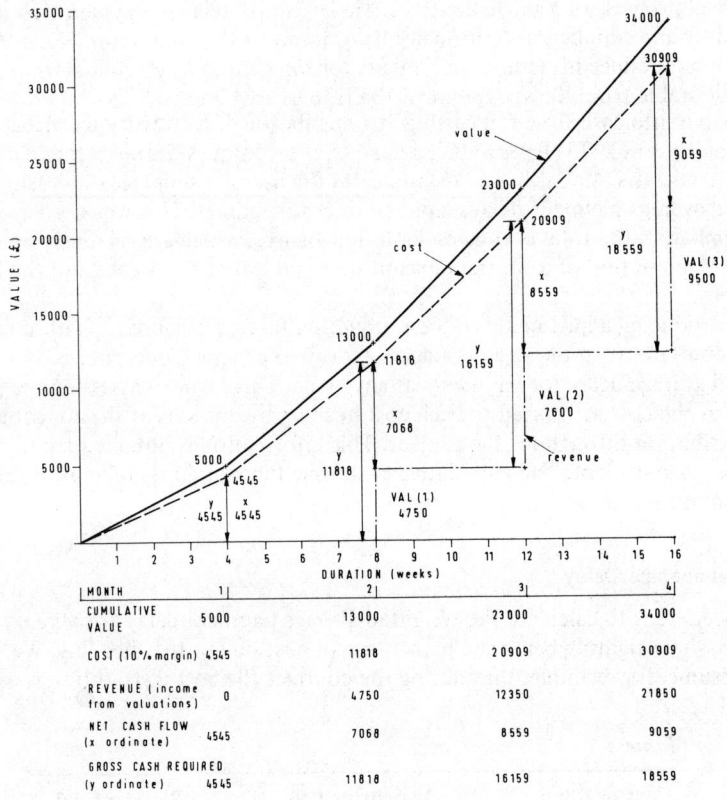

Figure 5.2   Cash flow—S-curve assessment, excluding delay

5.2 and 5.3 which give the relationship between time, value, cost commitment
and revenue. The 3-week delay in payment is plotted, and its relationship to the
revenue (income from valuations) shows a reduction in the cash commitment that
must be provided by the contractor so as to finance the work in progress. The net
cash-flow requirement is represented at the beginning of each month by the ordinate x and the maximum cash requirement by the corresponding ordinate y. The
commitment at the end of month 1 (week 4) will be a cash commitment for wages

Table 5.2

Month	Cash forecast	Cumulative revenue from valuation	Net cash flow	Monthly value released	Maximum cash requirement
1	4545	–	4545	–	4545
2	11 818	4750	7068	4750	11 818
3	20 909	12 350	8559	7600	16 159

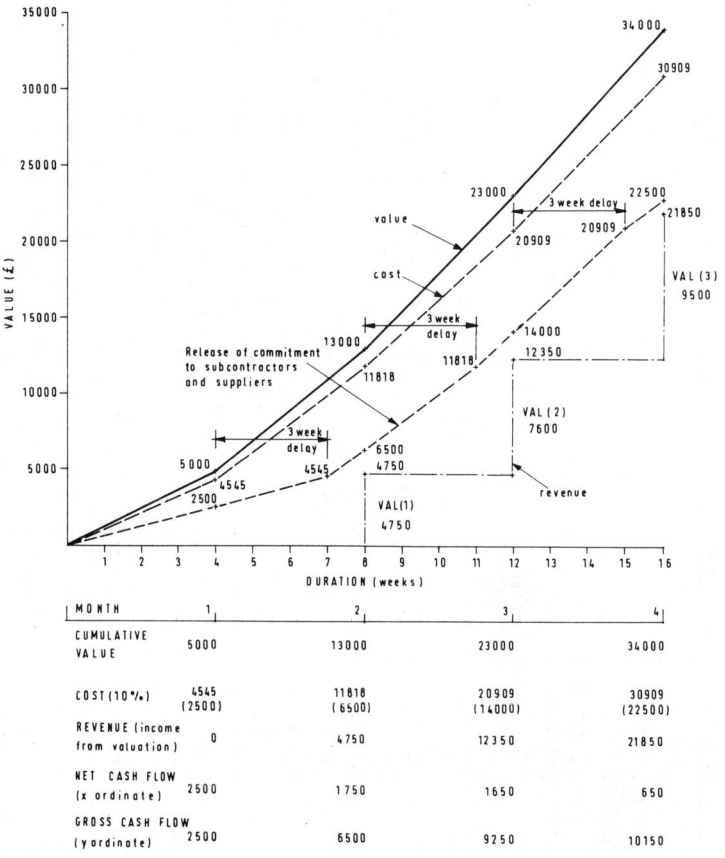

Figure 5.3   Cash flow—S-curve assessment, including 3-week delay

Table 5.3

Month	Cash forecast	Cumulative revenue from valuation	Net cash flow	Monthly value released	Maximum cash requirement
1	2500	—	2500	—	2500
2	6500	4750	1750	4750	6500
3	14 000	12 350	1650	7600	9250

paid in the employment of labour and this has been approximated on the diagram. Calculations indicate the effect on the cash flow by comparing figures with and without the effect of the 3-week delay. Figure 5.2 shows the cash flow, excluding the delayed-payment effect; the calculation of the maximum cash requirements is indicated in the cash-flow assessment in table 5.2. Figure 5.3 shows the adjusted

Operation Number	Operation	Month Budget	JANUARY (1)				FEBRUARY (2)				MARCH (3)				APRIL (4)				MAY (5)				JUNE (6)			
			1	2	3	4	5	6	7	8	9	10	11	12	13	14	15	16	17	18	19	20	21	22	23	24
1	SET UP SITE	9 000	9 000																							
2	REDUCED LEVEL EXCAVATION	14 600	7 300		7 300																					
3	DRAINAGE AND MANHOLES	16 500			4 000		6 250		6 250																	
4	ROAD BASE AND SUB-BASE	21 000							5 000		8 000		8 000													
5	ROAD SURFACING	9 700													4 850		4 850									
6	PUMPHOUSE EXCAVATION	2 800											2 000		800											
7	PUMPHOUSE BASE AND WALLS	12 200													3 050		3 050		3 050		3 050					
8	INTAKE CONNECTIONS	6 000																	3 000		3 000					
9	PLANT AND EQUIPMENT	16 000																	4 000		4 000		4 000		4 000	
	BUDGET		16300		11300		6250		11250		8000		10000		8700		7900		10050		10050		4000		4000	
	CUMULATIVE		16300		27600		33850		45100		53100		63100		71800		79700		89750		99800		103800		107800	

Figure 5.4 Programme—budget

cash flow, taking account of the delay. The corresponding cash flow assessment, taking the 3-week payment delay approximately into account, is as in table 5.3. Cash-forecast figures have been approximated from the delayed-payment curve.

The effect of the delayed-payment approximation is to reduce the cash-flow requirement considerably at the beginning and end of each month.

EXAMPLE 5.1

The master programme in figure 5.4 denotes the forecast of monthly and cumulative values throughout the contract period. Prepare a cash flow forecast for the contract based on the following payment delays and analysis of tender.

Month 1–3	*Proportion of total cost*
Labour	10%
Material	10%
Plant	70%
Subcontractors	10%

Month 4–6	
Labour	30%
Material	20%
Plant	30%
Subcontractors	20%

Payment delay in meeting commitment – after the end of the month in which payment is raised.

Labour	1 week
Materials	4 weeks
Plant	8 weeks
Subcontractors	2 weeks

Average delay simplification

Months 1–3

Labour	10% × 1 week	= 0.10
Materials	10% × 4 weeks	= 0.40
Plant	70% × 8 weeks	= 5.60
Subcontractors	10% × 2 weeks	= 0.20

Average payment delay   6.3 weeks
say, 6 weeks

Months 4–6

Labour	30% × 1 week	= 0.30
Materials	20% × 4 weeks	= 0.80
Plant	30% × 8 weeks	= 2.40
Subcontractors	20% × 2 weeks	= 0.40

Average payment delay   3.90 weeks

say, 4 weeks

Forecast of monthly and cumulative value from programme

The bar chart programme indicates the cumulative budget figures at time intervals of two weeks throughout the contract period.
Based on a profit release of $7\frac{1}{2}\%$ the cost assessment has been calculated, as follows.

Month	Date	Weeks	Cumulative value (£)	Cost forecast value × 100/107.5
1	Jan.	1–2	16 300	15 163
		3–4	27 600	25 674
2	Feb.	5–6	33 850	31 488
		7–8	45 100	41 953
3	March	9–10	53 100	49 395
		11–12	63 100	58 697
4	April	13–14	71 800	66 791
		15–16	79 700	74 139
5	May	17–18	89 750	83 488
		19–20	99 800	92 837
6	June	21–22	103 800	96 558
		23–24	107 800	100 279

Assessment of Income or Revenue from Interim Valuations

Month 1	Value forecast	27 600	
	Monthly release (cumulative)		—
Month 2	Monthly forecast	27 600	
	Less retention 5%	1380	
	Gross value	26 220	
	Less previous payments	—	
	Net monthly release		£26 220
Month 3	Cumulative forecast	45 100	
	Less retention 5%	2255	
	Gross value	42 845	
	Less previous payments	26 220	
	Net monthly release		£16 625
Month 4	Cumulative forecast	63 100	
	Less retention 5%	3155	
	Gross value	59 945	
	Less previous payments	42 845	
	Net monthly release		£17 100
Month 5	Cumulative forecast	79 700	
	Less retention 5%	3985	
	Gross value	75 715	
	Less previous payments	59 945	
	Net monthly release		£15 770
Month 6	Cumulative forecast	99 800	
	Less retention 5%	4990	
	Gross value	94 810	
	Less previous payment	75 715	
	Net monthly release		£19 095

Month 7	Cumulative forecast	107 800
	Less retention 5%	5390
	Gross value	102 410
	Less previous payment	94 810
	Nett monthly release	7600
	Add retention release 2½%	2695

£10 295

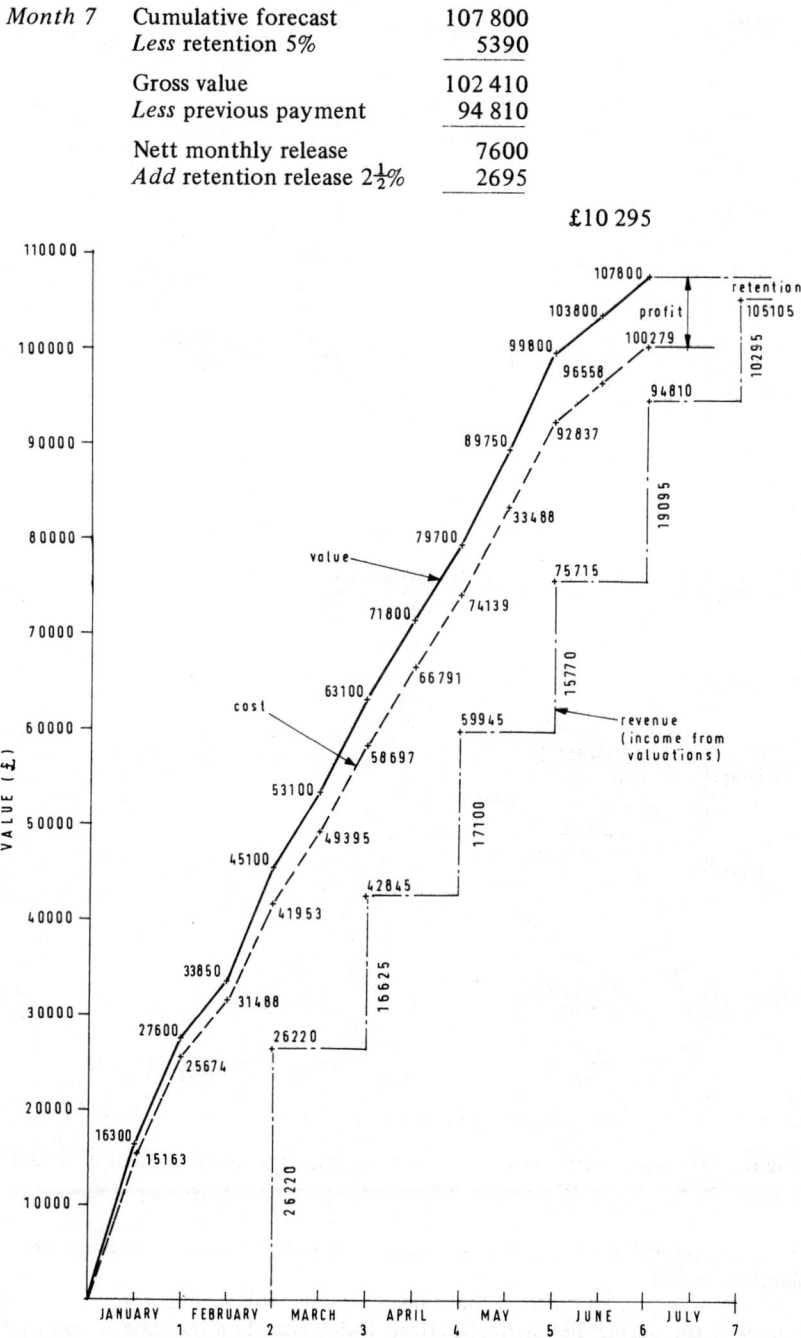

Figure 5.5 Value–time, cost–time and revenue–time curves—normal payment position

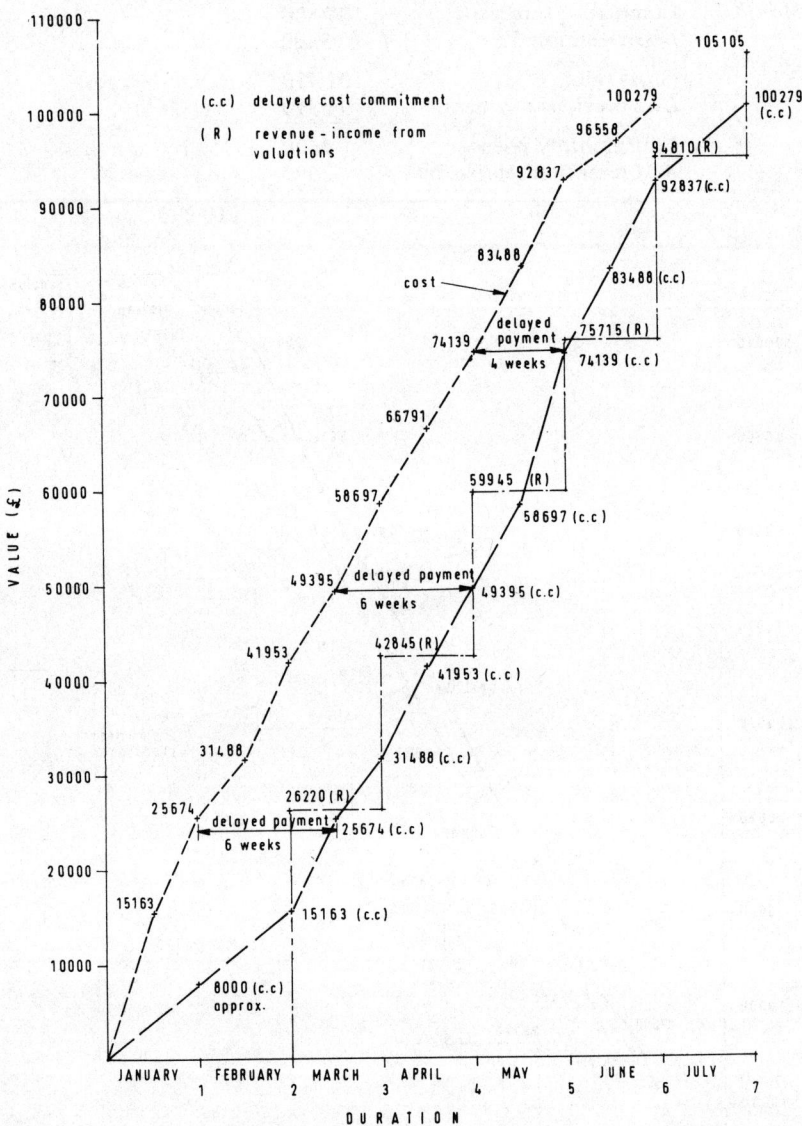

Figure 5.6   Value–time, cost–time and revenue–time graph—effect of delayed payments

A further retention release of £2695 will be raised at the end of the defects liability period.

The value, cost and revenue have been plotted against time in figure 5.5 to represent the normal payment situation. This is based on the assumption that all payments or cost commitments will be met within the month in which they were raised. Figure 5.6 indicates the effect of the delay in meeting the cost commitment. A delay of 6 weeks occurs in months 1–3 and a delay of 4 weeks

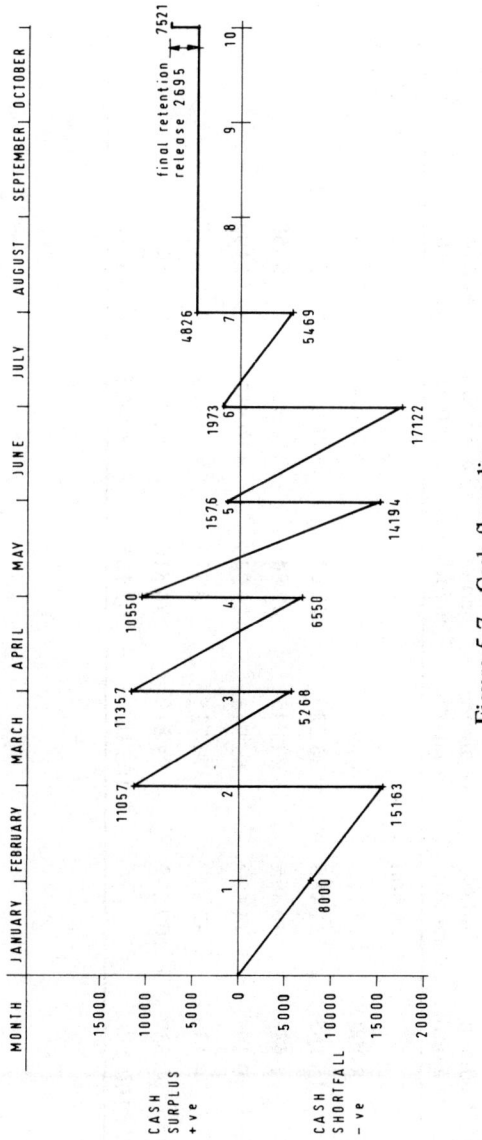

Figure 5.7   Cash flow diagram

Table 5.4

Month	Cost		Income		Cash-flow position		Notes
	beginning of month	end of month	beginning of month	end of month	beginning of month	end of month	
1	–	8 000	–	–	–	–8 000	The beginning of the month relates to the first day of the month
2	8 000	15 163	–	–	–8 000	–15 163	
3	15 163	31 488	26 220	26 220	+11 057	–5268	
4	31 488	49 395	42 845	42 845	+11 357	–6550	
5	49 395	74 139	59 945	59 945	+10 550	–14 194	
6	74 139	92 837	75 715	75 715	+1576	–17 122	
7	92 837	100 279	94 810	94 810	+1973	–5469	
8	100 279	–	105 105	105 105	+4826	+4826	

in months 4–6. This has the effect of moving the cost curve over a period of time corresponding to the delay. The delayed-payment curve intersects the stepped revenue diagram, resulting in a surplus-cash situation at certain time periods (positive cash flow) and a deficit position (negative cash flow) at other times.

The cash flow is shown more clearly in table 5.4 and graphically in figure 5.7. Harris and McCaffer (1977) have prepared similar cash flow forecasting examples on the basis of computer programs developed by Professor Trimble at Loughborough University of Technology.

References

Brown, R. G. S., *The Administrative Process in Britain* (Methuen, London, 1970).

Hardy, J. V., *Cash Flow Forecasting for the Construction Industry*, M.Sc. Project (Loughborough University of Technology, 1970).

Harris, F. and McCaffer, R., *Modern Construction Management* (Crosby Lockwood Staples, London, 1977) chapter 10.

Kerr, D., *Cash Flow Forecasting*, M.Sc. Project (Loughborough University of Technology, 1973).

McCaffer, R., Comments at the Institute of Building Seminar on Cash Flow Forecasting (1975).

McKay, I. B., *Cash Flow Forecasting by Computer*, M.Sc. Project (Loughborough University of Technology, 1973).

Parsons, G. T. E., *Setting the Scene*, Paper to the Institute of Building Seminar on Getting Paid (London, January, 1976).

Reynolds, P. J., and Hesketh, P., 'An Analysis of the Construction Industry', in *The Construction Industry Handbook* (M. T. P. Lancaster, 1973) p. 86.

Robertson, G. F., *The Problem Examined*, Paper to the Institute of Building Seminar on Getting Paid (Glasgow, March 18, 1977).

6 Monthly Cost Control Procedures

Cooke (1973), in a review of the use of cost control procedures, found that most medium-sized contracting organisations (that is, building firms employing 60-299 staff and operatives) applied a monthly form of cost control, relying very largely on the comparison of monthly cost and value to assess the profit or loss situation in the course of construction operations.

Few medium-sized organizations operate weekly cost control systems. Such systems reduce the dependence of the management on monthly cost–value comparisons for site control purposes, since operational costs are reviewed over shorter periods. Large organisations, which rely more often than smaller firms on weekly control systems, are also more remote from their sites and rely on financial statements produced from accounting data rather than on reports based on site cost information.

Financial control depends upon monthly cost–value comparisons. After internal adjustment, these may be presented in tabular monetary form or be expressed graphically for comparison with the contract budget forecast. The profit margin release per month or cumulative margin to date may be expressed in monetary terms or as a percentage. If, for control purposes, it is found necessary to introduce a weekly system, then this must be reconciled with the monthly account periodically. It is arguable that, if a control system discloses an unsatisfactory situation, the necessary remedial action can hardly wait until a monthly financial review. To act on the basis of an unreconciled report may prove to have been precipitate, but not to act until the monthly report could lead to irrecoverable loss. The solution, in this situation, is to set up parallel site control procedures, whether these are cost-based or not.

Objectives of Monthly Procedures

The exercise of financial control is a form of monitoring. It oversees financial performance without dwelling on the detail and, in its adverse reports, directs senior managers and directors to situations that appear to justify investigation.

An adverse financial account acts as a warning. The cost data collection system at site may respond with useful and reliable information that explains the situation. Even if it does not, transactions will have been made. Given a classification of the cost data in terms of the factors of production — labour, materials, plant and overheads — it should be possible to determine whether one of these is a particular source of loss, and so to direct the search for an explanation.

Beyond that point, the organisation and equipment of the firm will determine whether it will seek to obtain yet further detail from its site cost-control procedures, or instead rely, as most do, on various measures of physical control (which *indicate* productivity or utilisation as a *guide* to cost).

The objectives of such procedures are

(1) to derive from the accounting procedures of the firm a monthly indication of contract status, and
(2) to provide directors and senior managers with a guide to those activities of the firm that require their attention.

The limited detail and the necessity for further enquiry are reasons enough to emphasise the importance of speed in the presentation of such reports. They report on events that occurred, on average, two to three weeks previously. By the time the report appears the cause of a situation is likely to be a month old. To extend this time very much reduces the control effectiveness of the procedure.

Accuracy of Monthly Data

The liquidity of the company's funds depends upon the valuation of work done and the control of outgoings. It may be necessary to press hard for the one and delay the other. The figures are then not of liabilities and entitlements but of receipts and payments. To base the monthly report on the latter, without reconciliation, would be misleading.

The quantity surveyor is required

(1)   to reconcile the valuation to a common date;
(2)   to make adjustments for variations pending agreement;
(3)   to prepare an assessment of the increased cost element to date;
(4)   to assess items of daywork;
(5)   to assess the value of remeasured work sections that may influence the value of work undertaken.

An internal adjustment to the valuation must be undertaken within a period of seven days of the valuation date.

Ledger accounts and records prepared by the accountant must be in such a form that reconciliation with other information sources is possible. An assessment must be made of all goods received on the site up to the date of closing the ledger. Where invoices are outstanding for any goods delivered to site an assessment of the anticipated cost of the goods must be provisionally debited to the ledger. The ledger account should of course be checked carefully as an aid to reconciliation.

Cost–Value Comparisons – The Contractor's Surveyor's Responsibility

Cost–value comparisons are conveniently carried out monthly in the course of a contract, so as to coincide with the quantity surveyor's valuation in seeking an interim certificate.

The contract surveyor is responsible for producing the valuation data and, since this is to be used for cost comparison, it must be a fair estimate of the value of the completed work and not a factual statement of the lowest expectation (omitting variations, etc.).

The client's quantity surveyor is responsible for preparing the monthly payment certificates; in order to ensure that the contract is accurately valued, the contractor's surveyors should check the inclusion in the valuation of the following items.

Increased Costs

Increased cost returns for labour and material on fluctuation contracts must be submitted in sufficient time for inclusion in the account. Returns should be submitted monthly at least 7 days prior to the interim-certificate date in order that they can be checked and certified. Where the formula method is being applied the contractor should ensure the submission of all relevant documents.

The increased cost of material delivered to site and of labour will be included in the contractor's cost ledger. Gross errors in the assessment of the increased costs bear directly on the apparent profit or margin recovery.

Assessment of the Value and Agreement of Variations Issued

The tactics associated with variations and claims are affected by many factors, not least the character and attitude of those concerned. Variations should be agreed as they are carried out and included in the next valuation due if the outcome is to represent the situation properly.

Where this is not possible, it is desirable to include provisional assessment figures rather than omit such figures altogether. If these represent the minimum expectation from protracted negotiations then the contractor may not be aware of a substantial hidden value of variations during the contract. These only become apparent on settlement of the variations account towards the end of the contract or at the final-account stage.

However, costs incurred in carrying out variations will have been included in the labour and material costs, and will be reflected in the accounts.

Assessment of the Value of Dayworks

Similar procedures should again be adopted. Daywork sheets must be prepared weekly and signed, and their value is included in the next certificate.

Remeasured Work Sections of the Account

It is the contractor's responsibility to ensure that full documentation regarding remeasurement records are submitted to the client's quantity surveyor.

As soon as possible after completion of a bill section — say, substructures or drainage — a remeasure for the work should be submitted for checking and approval. This may then be included in the valuation.

Inaccuracy in Interim Valuations

Experience has shown that contractors tend to undervalue work in progress. Some of the areas of concern are as follows.

Assessment of Materials on Site

The materials on site should be valued for inclusion in the interim certificate. This will involve the careful checking of stockpiles of bricks, blocks, timber, frames and fittings.

To assist the accurate assessment of material on site, preprinted check sheets may be used. These should include basic material prices. The value of special items may be checked by reference to recent delivery notes. On large housing sites many thousands of pounds worth of goods may be stored in completed dwellings or garages. Appropriate time must be allowed for the correct assessment of the value of materials on site.

This appears to be one of the main sources of inaccuracy.

Assessment of the Value of Measured Work

The value of measured work may be assessed in various ways.

(1)   The value of bill items may be considered on an individual basis, item by item. On a large project this process tends to be laborious, and the surveyor may revert to valuing the percentage of each page completed.

(2)   The percentage value of each trade may be assessed. A more operational form of bill might simplify such assessment.

(3)   Schedules analysing the trades or operations to be carried out may be prepared. Individual blocks of flats or houses may be valued in lifts of brickwork, expressed as a percentage value of the trade section or measure for each house type. Simple tick sheets may be produced to simplify the valuation process. Undervaluation holds back monies until later stages of the contract and thereby distorts cost-value comparisons and controls based on them.

(4)   Contract preliminaries should be assessed carefully at each valuation stage. The value of each preliminary item may be reviewed to see whether the total sum may be released or only a proportion. The basis upon which to determine the proportion may be based on contract duration or on the percentage value of measured work.

Quantity Surveyor's Monthly Reports

In order that internal adjustments may be made to the valuation it may be necessary to submit a surveyor's monthly valuation report or progress report. This enables adjustments each month to be reviewed and compared. In the firm's reconciliation of the valuation it is necessary to ensure that something approaching the true value of work is compared with a realistic contract cost. Adjustments can be made for the following factors

(1)   under- or overvaluation of measured work sections;

(2)   variations to the contract that have been carried out but not yet agreed for inclusion in the account;

(3)   items of daywork undertaken but not agreed for inclusion in the account at the valuation date;

(4)   assessment of remeasured bill sections;

(5)   assessment of increased costs for the main contractor's labour and material;

(6)   adjustment of preliminaries for capital costs expended but not yet recovered.

Surveyor's monthly report			
Date/month ending	Val. No.	Contract.	
Valuation adjustment			
Description		Omit	Add
Valuation comparison		External valuation	Internal valuation
Preliminaries			
Measured contractor's work			
Variations to contract			
Materials on site			
Fluctuations: labour			
material			
Claims			
Domestic subcontractors			
Nominated subcontractors			
Nominated suppliers			
Gross valuation to date			
Less previous valuations at – – – – – – – – –			
Gross value for month			

Extension of time		Contract particulars	
Applied for		Contract com. date	– – – – – – –
Granted		Contract compl. date	– – – – – – –
Weeks ahead/behind programme		Duration	– – – – – – –
		Contract tender sum	– – – – – – –

Figure 6.1   Surveyor's monthly report

Quantity surveyor's monthly progress report				
Final account assessment		Date		
Final account		Surveyor		
Omit PC and P. sums.		Contract		
		Com. date		
Add anticipated value of PC and P. sums.		Compl. date		
Add Variations/inc. costs		Delay/ahead	weeks	
Anticipated final account total.		Fluctuations Material Labour		
Valuation details		Internal valuation at end of month	Agreed value at._ _ _ _ _ _	
Preliminaries				
Measured work on site				
Contractor's material on site				
Dayworks				
Increased costs				
Direct subcontractors				
N.S.C.				
N.S.				
Claims				
Variations to contract				
Summary of claims—description		Date notified	Ap value, £	Ag values, £

Figure 6.2 Quantity surveyor's monthly progress report

Figures 6.1 and 6.2 indicate suitable *pro formas* for presenting the surveyor's monthly valuation adjustments.

The surveyor's report also enables the claims situation to be reviewed along with any extension of time applied for and granted. A review of progress will indicate any delays to the contract — that is, weeks ahead of or behind the programme. The adjusted gross value indicated on the surveyor's report can be used for comparison with the actual cost situation, thereby permitting realistic comparisons and reviews of the contract's profitability in the course of the work.

Sources of Monthly Cost Data

The Accountant's Role

Accountancy staff are responsible for the record of transactions associated with the contract. Costs should be recorded in such a manner that reconciliation of liabilities and payments can take place at a given date each month. Figures that relate to an agreed valuation date (say the fourth Friday in every month) are required.

Payroll, transport and plant accounts will often be debited to the contract ledger account weekly.

Accounts for materials supplied to the contract, the payments of subcontractors and head office overheads will normally be debited monthly.

Sundry expenses for small purchases at site level — that is, weekly expenses for office and canteen, the purchase of small tools, Calor gas for office use and other such items — are charged as they arise, but may be paid directly or by monthly account paid one, two or more months after the receipt of the goods on site. This is dependent upon the supplier's promptness in submitting accounts and leniency with regard to credit, the credit rating of the contractor and the pressure on his liquid assets at the time.

At the date of reconciling the cost ledger, some allowance will have to be made for goods received on the contract for which invoices have not yet been rendered. An account of goods received during the month must be reconciled with invoices received for payment. Invoices not included in an account should be priced up at the quoted rates and a provisional sum entered in the cost ledger.

Both direct and nominated subcontractors should be instructed to make payment requests 7 days prior to the valuation date.

This will enable the account to be checked and included in the next valuation. After the valuation date the amounts requested by subcontractors must have been included in the valuation and debited to the contract ledger account.

The monies allocated in the valuation for a subcontract trade should be carefully checked against the subcontractor's invoice requesting payment. Overpayment to subcontractors can give rise to discrepancies, especially where the amount included in the valuation for the subcontractor is difficult to analyse and abstract from the bills of quantities.

The Contract Ledger Account

Cost data should be entered into the accounts ledger under headings appropriate for cost comparisons.

Cost centres or cost headings should

(1)   be related to activities that are readily identified;
(2)   be adaptable for comparison with monthly valuation data;

(3)   reflect expenditure on contract preliminaries, and
(4)   be identified with areas of expenditure on subcontractors, and specific units of labour and plant whenever possible.

Cost Centres for Ledger Account

The number of cost headings is required to be sufficient to meet the demands of those seeking information from the cost system.

The cost headings should aid the surveyor's monthly valuation analysis. The choice of cost headings in the ledger account should facilitate the quantity surveyor's reconciliation statement.

The following cost headings have been used for a simple ledger-accounting system in a medium-sized contracting organisation.

(1)	*Trade activities – labour*	Direct wages to operatives by trade; salaries — site management; payment to labour-only subcontractors
(2)	*Materials*	Direct materials debited to the contract
(3)	*Plant*	Plant-hire charges — outside hire; internal plant charges
(4)	*Preliminaries*	A selected number of different cost headings may be developed depending upon the information required by the company:
		(a) setting up site accommodation
		(b) telephone/heating
		(c) site-management salaries/expenses
		(d) scaffolding
		(e) sundry site expenditure/consumable stores
(5)	*Own subcontractors*	Payment to subcontractors directly employed by the contractor
(6)	*Nominated subcontractors*	Payments debited
(7)	*Nominated suppliers*	Payments debited
(8)	*Head-office overheads*	These may be charged separately to the contract or indicated in the ledger account
(9)	*Total cost*	

The ledger account must also contain information relating to the date of the entry, account or invoice reference/firm and amount invoiced. The accounts department may utilise their own system of invoice numbering but a coherent system of coding for the whole firm may reduce any possible confusion. Figure 6.3 indicates a cost ledger card statement for the allocation of construction costs.

Cost Ledger

Contract _____

Job No. _____

Date _____

Sheet _____

Date	Ref. details	Invoice ref.	Amount	Labour/ wages	Material	Plant.	Preliminaries			Own s/c.	N/S/C	N/S	H.O. overhead
							Site staff	Scaffolding	Temp./sun.				
		B/F.		Lab.									
		Total	cost	to:-							£		

Figure 6.3   Contractor's cost ledger

Procedure and Reconciliation at Monthly Intervals

At some date each month (such as the 28th day) the ledger account should be closed and totalled.

An assessment must then be made of outstanding invoices and entries to be included in the ledger, as follows.

(1)   The value of goods delivered to site for which invoices have not yet been received may be assessed by pricing delivery notes at quoted or current material rates.

(2)   The contractor's monetary commitment to subcontractors for work undertaken to date and included in the valuation must be assessed. Domestic subcontractors are frequently dilatory in their invoicing procedures, and the contractor must be vigilant if he is to avoid inaccuracy. High profit margins shown during the contract may be reduced dramatically when final accounts from subcontractors are received.

Cost-value comparison						
Month No.	Month			Date		
Contract No.	Contract	Value to date	Cost to date	Loss or profit £	%	Remarks
Notes						

Figure 6.4   Contractor's cost-value comparison

Cost and Financial Control for Construction Firms

Month	Monthly comparison of cost and value													Date
														Sheet No.
														Prepared by
	Value of contract	Contract	Month			Year to date			Contract to date			Profit loss, %	Retention held to date	Notes/action
			cost	value	profit/ loss	cost	value	profit/ loss	cost	value	profit/ loss			

Figure 6.5 Contractor's cost–value comparison

Entries in the valuation for nominated subcontractors and suppliers must be cross-checked in the ledger account. The quantity surveyor's monthly statement may show the contractor's commitments to subcontractors with any difference between monies included to date in the valuation and invoiced amounts requested by the subcontractor.

The accountant and the chief surveyor will compare the reconciled cost and value figures monthly. A cost-value report indicating the situation on all contracts in progress might be similar to the examples in figures 6.4 and 6.5, which provide a statement of the monthly and cumulative cost-value situation for presentation to the directors.

Figure 6.4 indicates the contract cost-value position to date on all contracts in progress. We go back to our introduction and point out that a 'loss' may be an expected deficit. Figure 6.5 enables the cost and value to be compared on a monthly, year-to-date and contract-to-date basis. The percentage profit or loss to date is indicated and also the current retention situation.

Monthly cost-value statement									
Contract					Tender sum Contract period Commencement date Completion date				
Valuation No.				Date					
Gross value certified Retention Increased costs Less previous payments Amount due				Gross value Gross value Inc. costs Adjustments Total			Variations Inc. costs Remeasures Claims Dayworks Other items		
				Adj. value			Adjustment total		
Subcontractor commitments									
Subcontractor	Amount included at bill rates	Margin %	Maximum commitments to subcontractor	Payment No.	Amount certified gross	Retention held	Amount certified net	Previous payments	Amount due
Comments									

Figure 6.6   Contractor's monthly cost-value statement

Monthly cost-value statement									

Contract   Heybridge lane   Preston

Tender sum	822 724
Contract period	78 weeks
Commencement date	1 April 1975
Completion date	25 Oct. 1977

Valuation No.   14   **Date**   2 June 1977

Gross value certified	518 923	**Gross value to**	May	
Retention 3%	15 568			
	503 355	Gross value	518 923	
Increased costs	52 236	Inc. costs	52 236	
	555 591	Adjustments	3100	
Less previous payments	507 043	Total	574 259	
Amount due	48 548			

Variations	800		
Inc. costs	1750		
Remeasures	400		
Claims	–		
Dayworks	150		
Other items	–		
Adj. value	574 259	**Adjustment total**	3100

Subcontractor commitments

Subcontractor	Amount included at bill rates	Margin %	Maximum commitment to subcontractor	Payment No.	Amount certified, gross	Retention held	Amount certified, net less $2\frac{1}{2}$%	Previous payments	Amount due
M & R Exc.	53 937	15	46 901	5	46 901	1407	44 357	43 500	1857
Morgan (Plast)	37 239	10	33 853	7	29 500	885	27 900	26 400	1500
Doon Concrete	7 246	10	6 587	3	6392	192	6 045	6 045	–
Cresta plumbing	33 000	10	30 000	8	30 000	900	28 372	28 372	–
N.W. Sealing	200	10	181	1	168	5	159	–	159
Marlway	12 000	10	11 091	2	7800	234	7 377	5 000	2377
Totals									

N.S.C./N.S.	Gross A/c	D/C							
Norton heating	14 888	$2\frac{1}{2}$	14 516	8	14 888	447	14 080	12 300	1780
N.W.E.B.	17 416	$2\frac{1}{2}$	16 981	2	17 416	522	16 472	14 720	1752

Comments

Figure 6.7   Completed cost-value statement

Monthly Cost Statement of Commitments to Subcontractors

In order to assess the commitment to subcontractors, both own and nominated, a monthly cost statement may be prepared at the valuation date. Figure 6.6 is one form of presentation, showing the contractor's monetary commitment to each subcontractor. These figures may later be used in developing the cost-value comparison. The amount due to each subcontract is derived from an analysis of the monthly valuation and clearly the subcontractor's certificate must not exceed this amount. If domestic subcontractors undervalue and thus fall behind with their payment requests, this is of benefit to the main contractor's cash-flow position but he must know the true liability involved.

Analysis of the subcontractor's quotation is necessary in order to assess the difference in margin between the main contractor's bill rates and the subcontractor's quotation. From this analysis the commitment to the subcontractor can be assessed. The statement enables the valuation adjustment to be estimated and the adjusted gross value to the month end to be shown.

Figure 6.7 shows a completed statement, illustrating its application in practice.

It must be emphasised that cost-value statements prepared at monthly intervals only indicate the over-all financial position at the date of the valuation. They are as accurate as the information available at the time. Further detailed analysis of the information is necessary in order to investigate the areas of profitability or loss. The data produced are mainly of benefit to senior management. Site control should have corrected situations before enquiries based on the monthly review reach the site.

Analysis of Monthly Cost Data by Management

The cost-value situation of contracts is reviewed monthly, not only as a form of production control but in order that the directors may decide on marketing strategy and any financial measure needed to ensure that resources are adequate. Action arising from the analysis of contract profitability will be delegated to the appropriate contracts manager in most cases. Apparent losses or reductions in profit margins that may cause the cash-flow position to worsen are the concern of the accountant.

Quite apart from confidence in its accuracy the cost-value comparison must be available as soon after the month end as possible in order that any action based on the analysis will be in time to be effective; if the analysis is of only historical value, then it reflects a control system without dynamism.

Research by Cooke (1973) showed that most companies relying upon monthly cost-value comparisons to provide profit data were able to produce the information within 7 to 10 days of the valuation data. Companies with weekly cost control procedures (either bonus- or planning-orientated systems) relied less upon monthly cost data for control information and comparisons took longer — up to 21 to 28 days after the valuation date.

Contractors' surveyors have to be aware of the purpose of the information they are producing and the need for accuracy during its collection and presentation. Surveyors should ensure that they value as accurately as possible and should refrain from holding monies back at the valuation stages. Accuracy of data and the speed of the analysis are the essential prerequisites of a monthly cost reporting system.

Action on the Basis of Monthly Cost-Value Comparisons

Where the cost-value comparison shows adverse trends, or where a loss in the month is reported, investigation is necessary. A director or the contracts manager would normally be delegated to the task of determining the source of the losses.

The investigation might consider the following aspects.

Analysis of Percentage Margin Release

Analysis of the profit or loss situation over the preceding months should identify any trends in profit or loss patterns. The analysis may show that percentage profits attained in earlier months are not being maintained. The presentation of the monthly percentage margin curve gives a useful guide to changes in profitability levels in the course of construction. An early decline in margins is a serious matter, since recovery in the later parts of the contract, except by claims, is unusual.

The percentage margin release curves in figure 6.8 illustrate this point.

Analysis of profitability levels achieved on a number of projects shows that an

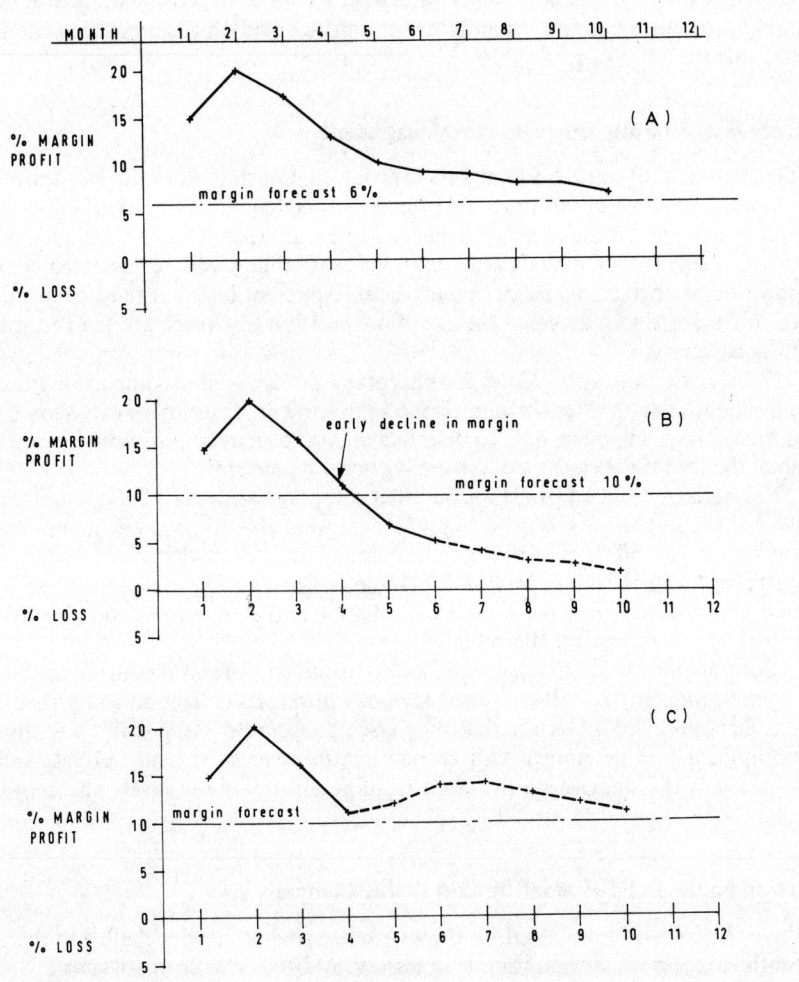

Figure 6.8   Analysis of margin release

early decline in margins highlights a need for investigation and action. Figure 6.8A shows a percentage margin release pattern similar to that observed on profitable contracts, the final profit release being marginally above the forecast margin. Figure 6.8B indicates a decline in margins early in the contract period and at month 5 the margin release has fallen below the forecast margin. Management investigation and action at month 4 might possibly result in an improved position, as indicated in figure 6.8C. It will be seen that, short of gross undervaluation, some extraordinary factor must be involved. Conversion of the data back to S-curve form would show how very unlikely such a recovery would be.

Accuracy of Cost and Value Data

The accuracy of the data on which the cost–value comparisons are based must be established. The first action of most experienced managers faced with a reported loss is to check the accuracy of both the valuation and the cost-ledger data. In practice, gross errors have been observed in these areas, especially in the buildup of the adjusted valuation figures.

Production Information Available from Weekly Cost Data

Where the company operates a production bonus system it has a measure of the productivity of individual trades or gangs. Individual operations, phases of work or trades may thus be shown to be less productive than others. Again, an experienced manager will first check the target rates.

Analysis of Labour, Plant and Preliminary Costs

The comparison of forecast values for cumulative labour and plant costs with actual values may suggest that attention should concentrate on one or the other. Trends are more valuable indicators of the situation than individual stage values. Underestimation of the preliminary items may occur when tendering. This, rather than mismanagement or irrecoverable variations in real cost, may give rise to loss.

Effectiveness of Site Management Team

The arbitrary removal of the manager of a contract that is recording a loss is not unusual. It allows losses thus far to be treated as history: the new man to have a fresh start and his seniors can be seen to have taken action. However, it is unlikely to lead to a significant improvement where bad estimating is the cause of the losses. A proper course of investigation is to analyse the problem and determine the action necessary to improve the position, preferably in an atmosphere free of the threat of retribution. Under threat the value of information may well suffer. The short-term planning facilities available to the site manager influence the use of resources. A weekly review of progress and plans for the following week permits direct action. Monthly cost-value comparisons are reporting past performance and few courses of action will be able to affect the current profit or loss situation.

Such courses of action can only hope to affect future cost–value figures. Cost-value reports can only become vehicles for production control decisions if the figures are adjusted to treat entitlements and commitments rather than monies paid and received. Smaller firms may resort to direct observation of managers, comparisons of actual and planned progress, and other such sources of information, which, if they all point to a worsening situation, provide a much more immediate warning that action is needed.

Mechanical data processing allied to reconciliation procedures may permit a production-control function to be based on cost–value reports. It would need to be accompanied by an objective system of accounting ascribing outgoings to specific production centres. Once the relevant production centre has been located, it should be possible to identify the cause of the loss and initiate corrective action – the two essential steps in any control procedure.

References

Cooke, B., *A Review of Cost Control Procedures in the Construction Industry*. M.Sc. Thesis (University of Manchester Institute of Science and Technology, 1973).

7 Weekly Cost Systems

A review of cost control procedures adopted by construction firms in the north-west of England (see Cooke, 1973) showed that weekly cost systems were used largely by the large contracting organisations. A lack of control standards within the majority of medium-sized firms (employing 60-299 staff and operatives) seemed to account for their reliance on monthly cost reporting to provide such profitability and cost data as was seen to be required. Within the medium-sized company there was little emphasis on cost reports and feedback. Fewer formal procedures were employed and it was considered that the introduction of a weekly reporting system would not necessarily produce a higher standard of control, especially without the management structure to support it.

When introducing or developing a system of cost control for a company, the following factors should be considered.

(1)   The system must be flexible: it may need to be extended so as to provide additional cost information as the company expands and the nature of its work changes.

(2)   The cost system is additional to the usual subjective accounting procedures of the firm, and its cost must be covered by perceptible benefits.

(3)   The cost information retrieved should be subject to periodic review. In practice systems have been observed to produce useless information week after week without this becoming a matter of concern. The production of detailed reports does not in itself ensure success.

(4)   The information gained from the control system must lead to the opportunity for corrective action. Without regulation to correct the reported situation there is no control.

(5)   The output of the system should be readily understood at all levels of management.

Within the construction industry no two firms operate the same cost system. This is due to the wide variety of work undertaken and the variability of management structures.

Systems of cost control are usually of one of the following forms

(1)   cost and bonus related systems;
(2)   short-term planning-orientated *or* pretarget-based cost systems;
(3)   operational cost systems.

Trade	Direct production cost set against target	Target value	Bonus, paid incentive guaranteed		Non productive costs	Total production cost including bonus	Bill value	Gain	Loss
Labourers	320	360	40	–	60	420	400	–	20
Bricklayers	395	460	65	–	30	490	540	50	–
Joiners	270	250	–	16	10	296	305	9	–
Excavator (mechanical plant)			–	–		160	80	–	80
			105	16	100	1366	1325	59	100
Preliminaries						220	180	–	40
			121			1586	1505	59	140
Summary								–	81

Figure 7.1   Extract from weekly cost report

Cost and Bonus Related Systems

Cost and bonus based systems are used by many large contracting organisations. The Working Rule Agreement (National Working Rules for the Building Industry — revised annually with local variations by each Regional Joint Committee) encourages contractors to offer an incentive bonus scheme. The bonus procedures are a direct source of information concerning the productivity of individual gangs or operations.

Information from the bonus system is available three working days after the week in which the information was recorded. This enables bonuses to be paid to the operatives one week later than earned.

Bonus data enable the time occupied by trades in specific tasks to be compared with targets at weekly time intervals; figure 7.1 indicates a weekly cost report produced from bonus information showing a summary of the total production costs (including bonuses paid) compared with the bill value of the work. Some firms work simply on time planned, expended and thus saved. This is converted to cost when the payroll is made up. This example shows that a bonus amounting to £121 has been paid out, even though the contract shows an overall loss for the week amounting to £81. There were losses on labour gangs, preliminaries and an item of mechanical plant. Additional costs have also been incurred on operations for which there is no bonus target.

It is clear that resources must be employed in checking timesheets daily and undertaking spot checks during construction operations. In this way the 'swinging of time' to items for which there is no bonus target can be checked and controlled. There is a conflict between the cost of operating a complex system and that of containing manipulation of a partial scheme. A company may target every operation, including the nonproductive items such as clearing site roads, cleaning up after other trades, denailing timber, unloading and distributing materials and attendance on other trades. But targets have to be agreed, and it may be difficult even to obtain data from which to establish some of the targets. Anomalies are meat and drink to a shop steward seeking to improve the wage levels of his men. In order to allow for such contingencies it may be necessary to provide a monetary allowance in contract preliminaries, and this could reduce competitiveness.

Problem areas associated with bonus systems are as follows.

(1)   It is necessary to control and check time records. Time transferred from operations that are subject to bonus payments to those that are not may inflate the bonus by reducing the time recorded for some other activity.

(2)   Care must be taken that bonus targets are realistic and acceptable to the operative and the firm. Targets should be based on work study, or on authentic historic cost data.

(3)   Accuracy of measurement is essential: measures recorded for bonus payment must be reconciled with the bill or quantity surveyor's measure at regular intervals. Gross errors can become apparent when comparing cumulative values measured for bonus payment with those recorded for valuation purposes.

(4)   Accurate and consistent feedback data from bonus systems are difficult to maintain. The accuracy of data is dependent on the correctness of time allo-

Cost and Financial Control for Construction Firms

cation to coded operations and the preparation of a true and representative measure. Unit-rate analyses have been observed to vary by up to 300% when comparing output data from similar operations occurring in different weeks.

Figure 7.2 presents a weekly cost statement related to site operations and preliminary items, showing the weekly and cumulative situation.

Figure 7.3 shows a further alternative cost statement in relation to the main phases of work on a housing contract. In this case the net percentage gain or loss per week has been expressed for each work stage, together with the overall percentage gain or loss to date.

Weekly cost statement Contract No. Contract		Week No.				Week ending	
Operation	Code	This week				To date	
		value	cost	gain	loss	gains	losses
External works		120	100	20	–	310	–
Drainage		96	120	–	24	–	120
Substructure–excavation		–	–	–	–	400	–
concrete		260	210	50	–	180	–
formwork		325	286	39	–	127	–
Superstructure–formwork		180	161	19	–	165	–
reinforcement		95	70	25	–	80	–
concrete		60	88	–	28	25	–
Total		1136	1035	153	52	1287	120
Preliminaries Attendance		60	85	–	25	85	–
Clean site		80	40	40	–	–	160
Unloading		60	75	–	15	–	120
Erect compounds		–	–	–	–	210	–
Total		200	200	40	40	295	280
Total of measured work		1136	1035	153	52.	1287	120
Preliminaries total		200	200	40	40	295	280
		1336	1235	193	92	1582	400

Figure 7.2   Contractor's weekly cost statement

Contract	Period ending				
Item	Costs		Results		Notes
	value	cost	gain	loss	
Productive work					
Foundation work					
Bulk excavation	180	110	70	—	
Drainage	140	165	—	25	
House foundations	240	210	30	—	
Mixer set up	90	60	30	—	
	650	545	130	25	Net gain 16%
Superstructure					
External brickwork	420	400	20	—	
Roof construction	180	210	—	30	
Roof tiling	85	80	5	—	
	685	690	35	30	Net loss 1%
Finishes					
Joinery first fix	180	160	20	—	
Joinery final fix	100	90	10	—	
Plumbing first fix	80	70	10	—	
Plastering	320	300	20		
	680	620	60	—	Net gain 9%
External works					
Garage foundation	110	90	20	—	
Drives and paths	60	95	—	35	Access difficult
	170	185	20	35	Net loss 3%
Preliminaries					
Site supervision	160	190	—	30	Ganger not allowed
Attendance	60	90	—	30	
Clean site	40	100	—	60	S.G. waggons
	260	380	—	120	Net loss 46%
Total this week	2445	2420	235	210	Net gain 1%
Total to date	16 801	14 791	4620	2610	Net gain 12%

Figure 7.3   Contractor's weekly cost statement

Short-term Planning Orientated or Pretarget Based Cost Systems

Production control systems that integrate cost control and short-term planning procedures have been developed. The objectives of a planning–cost orientated system of control are as follows

(1)   to incorporate into a single integrated control system the functions of production planning, cost control and value control;

(2)   to set productivity targets, the achievement of which will result in a specified bonus return and so reduce the complexity to a single term (once these targets are agreed there are no details to pick over);

(3)   to determine where, why and how the actual margin varies from the planned margin in relation to the stages of work;

(4)   to relate the bonus to the progress of the site as a whole, and obviate anomalies in the bonus paid to different gangs and trades (trades that are used to high earnings on a task-target basis tend to resist job-bonus systems);

(5)   to reduce overheads associated with measurement by limiting this to progress forecasting and measurement, which may also serve for valuation purposes.

A system such as this would benefit from a more operational form of billing. The basic principles of a cost–planning orientated system are illustrated in figure 7.4, which shows the relationship between planned cost and the planned and actual value released per week.

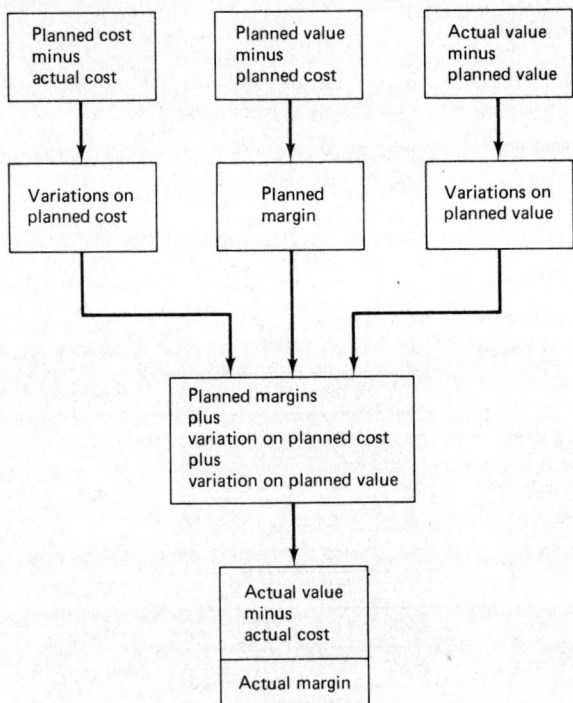

Figure 7.4   Principles of cost–planning orientated cost system

The general principles of operating the system may be considered in four categories: planning, value, cost and margins.

In the context of *planning*, the operating principles are as follows

(1)   to break down the work content of the contract into identifiable and measurable operations that correspond to short-term planning;

(2)   to assess the resources required for labour, plant, materials and time in which to complete the operations;

(3)   to synthesise these operations into a time-based construction programme and therefore to exercise control by comparing actual progress with planned progress.

As regards *value*, the appropriate operations are as follows

(1)   to establish for each operation the planned value (quantity of work to be performed times bill rate) and then, at regular intervals, the planned value of work to be done in order to keep on programme;

(2)   to exercise value control by comparing, weekly and monthly, the planned value with the actual value.

The operating principles relating to *cost* are as follows

(1)   to determine for each period the planned cost of labour, plant and site overheads (the planned cost is the sum of the estimated cost of these factors allocated to the various operations for the period – a week – to which the planning relates);

(2)   to exercise cost control by comparing planned and actual costs.

Finally, the principles relating to *margins* are as follows

(1)   to determine for each operation a planned margin and therefore a contract-planned margin (the planned margin is the planned value minus the planned cost for a particular programmed period);

(2)   to determine at monthly and weekly intervals the contract margin attained by the application of value and cost control with respect to the variations from planned value and planned costs.

Operational Cost Systems

The principle of operational costing is to issue a complete job instruction in the form of a job card. This may be of a form not unlike that proposed by the N.F.B.T.E. in its publication *Business Procedures for the Small Building Firm.* There are other more detailed forms that incorporate a check list of plant, materials and instructions (drawings and specifications).

The principle is that a record of time spent and goods received should be recorded on the back of the card. When the job is complete this then contains a full account of plan and achievement.

This system, in one form or another, is particularly appropriate for jobbing and specialist firms. Clearly, if the work embraced is too extensive or complex, the system fails. There are instances, however, when the combination of a job-card instruction and record at gang level might be beneficially incorporated into a larger scheme.

EXAMPLE 7.1

A Weekly Cost–Planning Orientated System

The example presents the detailed procedures adopted for weekly short-term planning and illustrates the relationship between site planning activities over a three-week period during which the planning and cost results are analysed. The application of these procedures enables the contract progress to be assessed and, by premeasuring the programmed work, the cost of performing the work

Preplanning period. Budget or plan prepared one or two days prior to the work period.

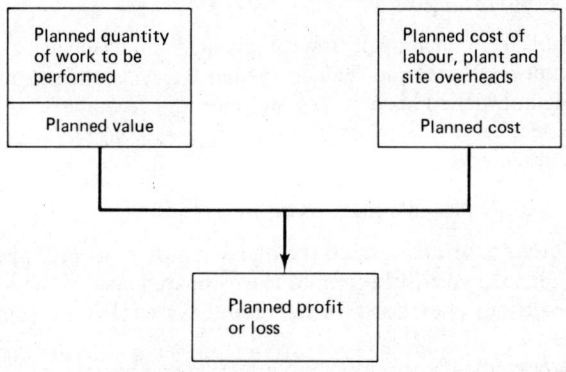

Working period (1 week). Work schedule carried out in accordance with the short-term planning. Progress updated at the end of each day—adjustment if necessary to cope with short-term requirements.

Measurement of actual work performed

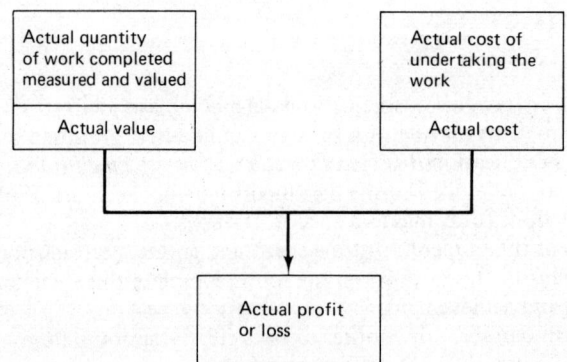

Analysed data available three days after working period.

Figure 7.5   Principles of weekly cost–planning system

Weekly site plan of work

Week No.
Date

Estimated measure and programme of work from . . . to . . .

Contract Labour gang.		Plant allocated	Monday	Tuesday	Wednesday	Thursday	Friday	Saturday	Sunday/Remarks
Labourers gang 1 drainage	4	JCB AC 50 m pump	Excavate drains mh 8-12 Lay and joint pipes		Concrete bases to manholes. Surround to drain runs.		Excavate m.h. 14-15	Fix m.h. rings	
Concrete gang	3	Vibrator	Concrete floorbays $1-4 to 8		Columns C20 to C28	Blinding to floorbay 10 and 12	Conc. 1st floor beams $1		
Bricklayers gang 1	6 b.l. 3 lab.	Mixer Dumper		External wall flooting $1-6.		M.hs. F1 to 4.	Ext. wall $1 to 2		
Carpenters gang 1	3c 1 lab		Make beam sides $6	Fix fwk to cols. C20-C28	Fix fwk ground beams $7.	Strip fwk to cols C20-25	Make beam sides $6		
Scaffolder	2s		Erect scaffold to external wall $1 and 2		Erect scaffold $6	Erect scaffold to beams	External wall $1 and 2		
Total labour	22								

Site manager

Figure 7.6 Weekly plan of work

Contract			Plan			Actual			W.E. date Week No.	
Bill ref.	Description	Target rate—labour and plant	Measure	Value (£) Lab. and plant		Measure	Value (£) Lab. and plant	Remarks	Cost summary	
									details	plan	actual
									Wages		
									Labourers		
									Bricklayers		
									Carpenters		
									Scaffolders		
									Site administrator/foreman		
									Add %		
									Plant		
									Site on cost		
									Supervision		
									Cabins		
Total labour and plant value			Gain or loss			Gain or loss			Total cost		
Deduct total cost										

Weekly cost control

Figure 7.7   Weekly cost statement

can be analysed weekly. By this means, sections of work that are behind programme are reviewed at weekly intervals and resources may be made available
to ensure that planned progress is maintained.

The principles of the system are outlined in figure 7.5. Analysis of the results enables planned and actual profits or losses to be matched and this enables
the site management to assess the feasibility and effectiveness of their short-
term planning procedures employed on site. Feedback information is available
three days after the period in which the work was undertaken.

Figure 7.6 shows the format utilised for presenting the short-term weekly
planning. Figure 7.7 shows the weekly cost report, which enables the planned
and actual cost and value to be matched.

The implementation of the weekly control system involves the following
stages.

Stage 1   Preparation of the Weekly Site Plan

On the Thursday or Friday of each week a weekly site planning meeting is
convened to prepare the weekly site plan of work (figure 7.6). This meeting
will be attended by the site manager, general foreman, trades foreman and
gangers. The site measuring surveyor or quantity surveyor will also attend.
He will be responsible for converting the weekly programme into a planned
value based on the premeasurement of the work to be undertaken. Where a
single production control unit is employed this task would be a joint responsibility.

Weekly planning should be based on the requirements of the monthly or
six-weekly programme objectives. This will ensure that operations behind
programme are given preference and kept under constant review. Obviously
every effort will be made to make the most of available resources. Three copies
of the weekly plan of work are compiled for distribution to the trades foremen,
general foreman and site manager.

Stage 2   Preparation of the Weekly Cost Control Sheet

The work indicated on the weekly site plan is premeasured and valued by
applying the estimated labour and plant rates available from the analysis of
the bill. This is prepared on the Friday of each week and compared with an
assessment of the forecast weekly cost of wages and plant and site costs.
Forecast costs are based on the charges incurred during the previous week
and are normally available from site records of labour and plant expenditure.
Figure 7.7 suggests a form in which the forecast gain or loss for the programmed
work may be assessed. The weekly site plan may then be adjusted, if necessary,
to obtain an adequate earnings–spending balance. Copies of the weekly cost
control sheet are distributed to the site manager, contracts manager and head
office.

During the following week the programmed work set out on the weekly
site plan is carried out and updated and daily planning is implemented by site
management. Progress is recorded daily and the plan of work for the forthcoming week is again formulated on the Thursday or Friday.

Stage 3   Measurement of Work Performed

On the Monday following the week in which work was completed, the work
is measured by the site measuring surveyor. It is then valued at the labour and
plant rates indicated on the schedule and entered onto the weekly cost control
sheet. This enables the actual value of work completed to be assessed and com-

pared with the planned value. The surveyor and site manager are responsible
for assessing the validity of the planning. The reasons for any deviation from
the planned and actual margins can be reviewed during the assessment of the
following week's programme.

On the Wednesday of each week accurate data relating to the actual expenditure incurred in carrying out the work will be available. This relates to
wages paid, plant charges available from plant returns and actual site-overheads
expenditure. This enables actual margins to be compared with planned margins.

Contracts indicating satisfactory planned and actual margins can be assumed
to be adequately controlled by site management. By the implementation of
short-term planning procedures related to the premeasurement of planned work,
the cost and value of variable short-term programmes may be matched.

Where the planned cost appears to exceed the achievable value then the
extent of work to be undertaken to achieve a breakeven situation must be
assessed. Construction methods and the target rates are brought into question.

Feedback Data from the System

The direct relationship of a specific measure of work on the one hand to an allocation of time to plant and labour on the other permits unit-rate figures to be
reviewed and fed back to estimators and planners. Such a system depends upon
the maintenance of effective materials control, since the cost of works may be
found to offset some plant and labour savings by wastage or utilisation losses in
materials.

The importance of the individual timesheet is substantially reduced if such control systems are adopted. A timeclock suffices to identify working hours. Some
gangs may be entitled to overtime, as may labourers starting early to lay out equipment for craftsmen; however, such necessary arrangements can be incorporated in
agreements on the site conditions of work and payment without it being necessary
to maintain details of individual time records. Random cost checks can be set up
in the course of site operations to feed back production cost data in the event of
any specific requests for such information.

It is necessary to remark that the weekly progress target and the corresponding
bonus are offered for the agreement of the operatives. If the amount paid in a
series of weeks attracts dissatisfaction then there is pressure on stewards to take
issue over the extent of planned work and the return. Once it becomes necessary
to break down by trades and quantities and argue the bonus rates then anomalies
appear and the problems of negotiation escalate. There is much to say, therefore,
for a judicious approach to offers, particularly when men are becoming used to a
series of repetitive work tasks.

If such systems work well, there are benefits in morale from a common aware-
ness of task and reward.

EXAMPLE 7.2

A Weekly Cost–Planning Orientated System

This example illustrates the operation of a planning system based on premeasurement. A programme of work is prepared at site level, and is presented in bar-

chart form. The work content indicated on the programme is premeasured and valued at agreed target rates. Planned values are then matched against the planned cost in order to arrive at a forecast margin.

The example concerns the construction of a reinforced concrete culvert, as shown in figure 7.8. The short-term programme in figure 7.9 is a typical extract from a week during the erection of the culvert walls. The programme has

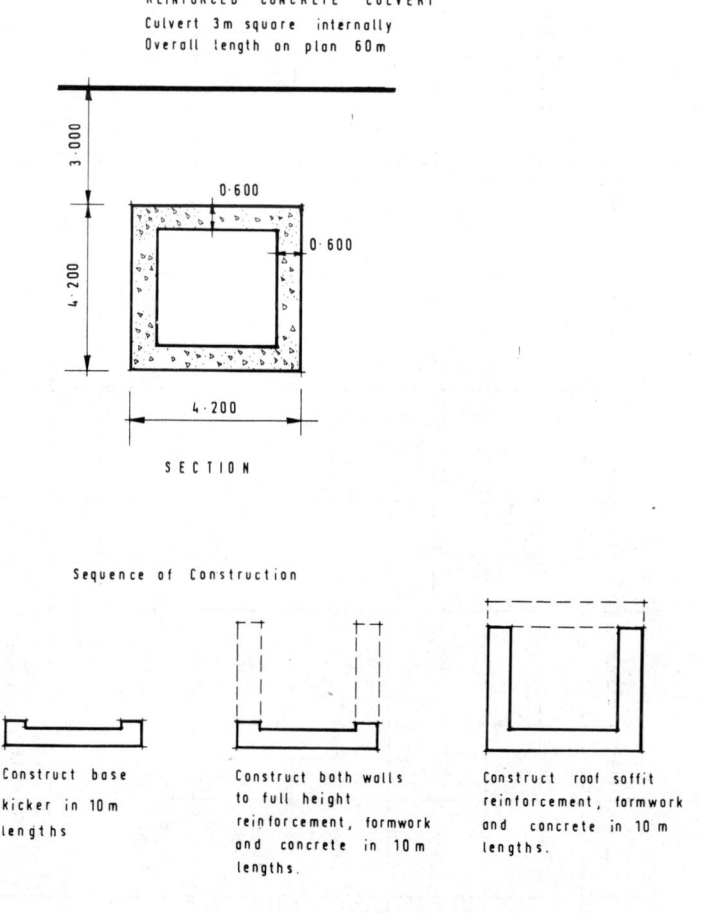

Figure 7.8   Reinforced concrete culvert

been prevalued and matched with the forecast cost of labour, plant and site overheads. This shows a planned net margin of £178.40 based on the planned programme of work. The firm's profit is included in its valuation figures.

The programme is prepared on the Friday of each week, at the weekly site planning meeting, and premeasured and valued the same day. An assessment of the cost is prepared on the basis of the labour, plant and site overheads in the previous week's records, adjusted for changes in labour and plant content.

Short-term programme

Week No.
Week ending

No.	Operation	Labour	Plant	Monday	Tuesday	Wednesday	Thursday	Friday	Sat.	Measure	Rate	Value
1	Erect formwork walls	2 Carp. 1 Lab.	22 RB		120 m²				120	240 m²	2.50	600
2	Rfs. to wall	2 S/F	—							8 ton	£30/ton	240
3	Concrete walls	3 Lab.	22 RB							18 m³	5.0	90
4	Make fwk to roof	2 Carp. 1 Lab.								90 m²	1.0	90
5	Strip formwork	2 Carp. 1 Lab.								120 m³	0.50	60
												1080

Remarks

Prepared by

Cost assessment

Labour			Plant		Site O/H		
2 Carpenters	48 h 1.80	172.80	22 RB.	150 —	Gen. fm.	110 —	
1 Lab.	48 h 1.60	153.60	Vibrator	12 —	Site plnr	50 —	
2 S/F	48 h 1.80	172.80	Bar bender	24 —	Cabins, etc.	18 —	
3 Lab	8 h 1.60	38.40		£186		£178	
		537.60					

Cost assess 901.60
Value asses 1080.00

Profit or loss 178.40

Figure 7.9   Prevalue and measurement of programme

The planned margin may be offered to the various operative gangs in the form of a bonus incentive payment. The proportion of the distributed surplus may be negotiated so as to be less than the whole, in order to retain funds for distribution in times of inclement weather or operational difficulty.

References

Cooke, B., *A Review of Cost Control Procedures in the Construction Industry*. M.Sc. Thesis (University of Manchester Institute of Science and Technology, 1973).

8 Specialist Contracting

There are special skills and areas of expertise which, in the normal course and sequence of contracts, would be called upon for too limited a time by any one firm to permit continuity of employment. Few large firms do their own plastering and painting, for instance. By forming companies to subcontract such work it becomes possible to enhance the lessons of experience on the one hand and to offer job security on the other.

There are also activities within construction, but not exclusive to it, which call upon resources and skills outside the contractor's range of expertise. Ornamental ironwork (blacksmiths) and various types of service installation (electricians, gas fitters, sheet metal workers, etc.) are cases in point.

Where such firms are associated with the contractor and the financial control of their activities has to be included in the budgeting process for a group of companies, it becomes necessary to understand how the process of costing differs from that familiar to those in construction contracting.

There are labour-intensive activities. At the extreme of the range is the labour-only subcontractor. Such subcontractors offer a product for a price rather than their skill and effort on the basis of a time rate. The criterion of acceptability is in the product, and the subcontractor's income depends on acceptance. Control is a matter of quality on the main contractor's part and of progress on the subcontractor's part. The difference between income and cost is often nothing to do with time but rather with an agreed apportionment of the proceeds. If the subcontractor were to introduce any form of control system—and this is rare, since in many cases the subcontractor is in effect a partnership of those concerned—then it would be a planning-based system.

On the other hand when men are engaged on a time basis, some control based on output standards is possible. Most such trades are connected with finishings. At that stage of construction work it is usual to adopt a cycle time within which each subtrade should complete its work on a storey or a phase, and allow the following trade to have working access. Manning is adjusted for completion in the cycle time. Once again, there will be a state of progress at some manning level that constitutes profitable working, and both for cost-control and incentive-bonus purposes this is the useful reference datum.

Capital-intensive operations tend to occur in manufacture, assembly and installation of components or equipment. Here sales revenue may be determined by the throughput of equipment, which depends on manufacture, distribution and installation, and these factors themselves may be interdependent. The rate of throughput that corresponds to profitable working may be identified by breakeven analysis.

Breakeven Analysis

Land, buildings, administration, marketing, upkeep and maintenance costs must be accepted if conditions in which production may take place are to be established. The volume of production does not affect these costs, unless it is such as to require the purchase of additional facilities or to permit the release of existing ones. Plotting cost against output leads to a graph as in figure 8.1 or a stepped curve.

On the other hand labour is in some instances paid on a piecework basis, that is, in direct proportion to output (figure 8.2). On other occasions time rate labour does not vary with output until an incentive bonus becomes payable or overtime is worked, when figure 8.3 would illustrate the situation.

Power to machines and materials to be processed will relate fairly closely to output, again producing a graph similar to figure 8.2.

Total cost, taking the simple case of piecework, will be as shown in figure 8.4. (Curve CC is the sum of FF in figure 8.1 and PP in figure 8.2).

Now the firm can expect to receive a revenue directly related to the number of its products delivered or installed. Unless the revenue rises more rapidly than cost, the enterprise must fail. If then we draw a graph of finance against output, costs being CC and revenue being RR, we arrive at figure 8.5.

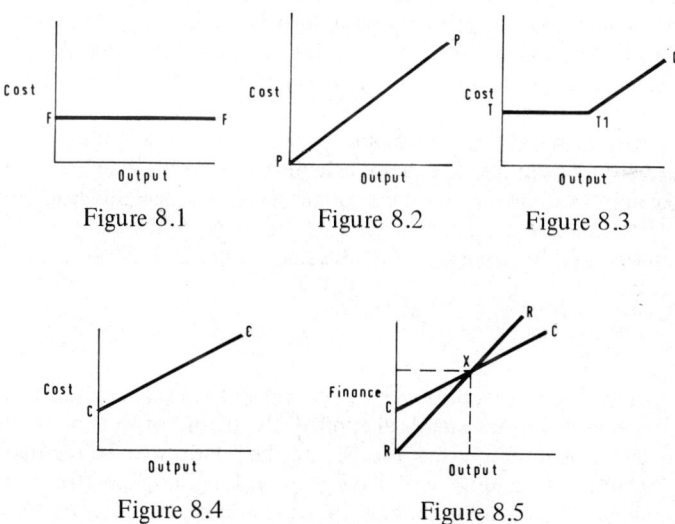

Figure 8.1 Figure 8.2 Figure 8.3

Figure 8.4 Figure 8.5

At some point X the activity breaks even and the ordinates between XC and XR show an increasing profit as output rises.

The output that earns revenue is determined by the number installed and approved, which means that failure to achieve output may arise from problems associated with quality or quantity. Failures in manufacturing, distribution, storage or the rate of satisfactory installation may be responsible. The value of a breakeven chart is that it helps to identify an acceptance-rate target that will enable some planned level of profit to be achieved. A rise in materials wastage or rejected work can eat into the profit margin. Rectification of defects within the period of warranty can also reduce the actual return.

It is clear, therefore, that experience of contingency margins as well as profit margins helps in establishing a target representing the breakeven point. Furthermore, to build up such a model demands past experience and a record of the production of comparable products, distributed over a similar distance, and assembled in comparable conditions. Given these, however, it is possible to develop a control standard that is distinguished by its simplicity and is a useful first indicator of performance. Such simplicity tends to be rare on construction sites.

Budgetary Control (Manufacturing)

Whereas in general contracting the phasing and magnitude of effort is only marginally susceptible to manipulation, there are benefits of production economy in long manufacturing runs. These may be contrived by ignoring the phasing dictated by strict attention to order and concentrating on maximising batch sizes. However, production economy of this kind must be weighed against the additional cost of warehousing until the materials are called up. Manufacturers who have no responsibility for assembly are tempted to deliver as produced and leave the storage problems to site. However, it is clear that short-term planning, aided by a marketing effort arising from budgeting exercises, can influence the profitability of such firms. The point here is that budget updating must take place within the currency of the order–delivery period so that marketing effort can be applied to produce some levelling of demand.

In repetitive manufacture the amount of material, the rate of power consumption, and the time of processing can be established to within fine limits. Work study can reduce actions to margins of milliseconds and, with due allowance for concentration and training, a rate can be agreed on the basis of an output of one unit in a given time period. Relating payment to such standards is termed *standard costing*.

Standard Costing

It is firstly important to recognise that, over time, a job must remain essentially the same with regard to the standard applied, the nature of workpiece, the nature and sequence of operation in the process and the relationship of the operative to the task (in terms of training, workplace geometry, lighting, comfort, etc.). To apply such standards in any other conditions would be an invitation to turbulence in labour relations. Furthermore, in such situations, peace is usually restored only on the basis of some compromise based on subjective judgements, and departure from strict observation, record and analysis may invalidate the procedure.

Given continuity and agreement, however, each of the variables can be allotted a cash value

(1)   price of materials—from quotations or invoices;
(2)   materials (cutting and waste)—from records;
(3)   labour—as negotiated, unit value based on output to achieve some target, possibly obtained by breakeven analysis;

(4)   plant—power and consumables, maintenance and spares based on records, output as for labour;

(5)   overheads—charges to be allocated to cover the running costs of the factory.

If costs are allocated in a similar manner, comparison between planned and actual values becomes possible. The source of differences can be located and investigated.

Spurious standards create dangers of misallocation of time to benefit by slack values and of anomalous comparisons, which may be used to leapfrog rates, and in other ways induce the decay of the control system. The history of incentive bonus schemes is littered with the bones of sacrifices to compromise. The more detailed the items and their values and the slacker the job descriptions, the more vulnerable such schemes have proved to be. It is a truism that output is as much a matter of attitude and morale as it is of muscle and movement; hence it is clear that good labour relations must be established before any success with standard costing is likely to be achieved.

Control Systems

By their nature, most subcontracting jobs are short-term. (The exceptions are mechanical and electrical service installations; we will discuss these later.) A cost-based control system may well be unable to report in time for a significant change to be made in site organization. A projection is required to establish an acceptable level of progress, and control can then be based upon its achievement and the resources needed to ensure it. Analytical techniques of work study and planning are then of more immediate relevance than cost control.

Much of the cost of mechanical and electrical installations, on the other hand, is in materials. A great deal of the fabrication having been done off-site, the site preparation and installation depend for their economy on job organisation and the elimination of materials lossess and wastage rather than on the output of labour.

The acceptance of service systems depends upon the commissioning process. Any systems of coding must permit the costs of fault rectification to be debited retrospectively to the tasks concerned.

We discuss such control systems later in the context of design and supply services. On other occasions the same contractor may install equipment designed and specified by a consultant. Materials storage and control are likely to be crucial to the successful completion of the work, but the manner in which the installers go about their work is important. However, when equipment is designed and installed, it is necessary that the site cost of design failures should be capable of determination. A firm may therefore need a control system that can be operated at different levels of detail.

Quantity surveyors may be more ready to offer billed items in relation to plumbing than to heating or electrical installation. Thus site cost control may be sufficient in the first case, whereas a more complex system may be needed in the second.

Design and Supply Contracting

The design of some fittings, installations or finishings may involve special technology and experience, which are not within the competence of the generalist
designer, be he architect or consulting engineer.

There are degrees of control that relate to the specifying capability of the
principal designer or client. Specification by performance and the inclusion of
provisions for some degree of warranty offer the possibility of competition based
on the cost and behaviour in service of the alternative products on offer. On the
other hand, to describe a product by materials, composition, condition and
standard tests leaves the responsibility for performance in the hands of the speci-
fier. If a product is supplied as stated but is unsatisfactory, rectification becomes a
call on contingency funds, and the benefit gained by the client from any competition is eroded.

If neither of these control procedures is adopted, price is apt to reflect areas of
ignorance or unscrupulousness. To design down to a price rather than towards some
optimum level of performance and price is simply to invite the client to accept the
worst of both worlds. It is clear that either lack of confidence or lack of detailed
knowledge may impel the designer to seek association with expert advisers. Either
the client may be advised to engage a specialist consultant or he may be recommended
to accept nomination or, at the most, limited competition, so that his advisers
may call on the design expertise of the selected supplier.

Often, as much as 40 per cent. of the value of the contract is sublet to specialists.
Since client financial control is directed, through the designer, toward the over-all
cost, the exercise of economy bears unevenly. To avoid an escalation of contract
costs there is little to do but to contrive some omission in the works, and as a
result specialist work, which tends to come late in the contract, faces alterations
and omissions as an ever-present threat. It is the controls and finishes rather than
the bones of the installation which tend to be affected. The principal components
will have been ordered and there is little choice but to modify the remainder, often
at the expense of appearance and flexibility.

A strong bond of interdependence established between generalist and specialist designers sets up a working relationship at a level that, in terms of influence,
is well above that of agent–clerk of works, at which the day-to-day business of the
designer and main contractor is conducted.

The framework of roles and relationships established by the contract form and
procedures—the 'formal system' as the Tavistock Institute of Human Relations
researchers called it—differs widely from the informal links and contacts maintained by individuals in the various organisations. It tends to be the latter which
open up the use of contingency funds when dealing with alterations and variations.

In the absence of a fully detailed design a provisional sum suffices in most
tender documents issued to firms competing for the main contract. Indeed Kelsey
(1974) states that, in mechanical contracting, when the order is received, and
detailed drawings and manufacturing and purchasing orders have been made out, a
revised estimate must be prepared. Financial control must be based on the original
quotation, but immediate variances, largely attributable to design and estimating,
are thus brought into relief. It is obvious that some such variances may be absor-

bed rather than be maintained as if they related to a fully documented bill, and competing specialist contractors can be expected to include an adequate allowance for contingencies. Some part of the competition is thus speculative rather than factual.

In a field of competition limited to experienced firms of some reputation the situation is one of oligopoly rather than perfect competition. The subcontract market is different in character from the construction market. Agreement relates to a complete product or service, whereas in general the main contract deals only with assembly.

In subcontract work there is an opportunity for a cost system reaching back into matters of design and organization. In other words there is a feedback loop capable of influencing the future behaviour of estimators and designers, as well as that of managers of production, distribution and site works. The specialist contractor is not subject to the constraints that prevent the main contractor from developing a fully effective control system. Indeed, the specialist contractor should perhaps be showing the generalists how effective control systems may be established.

There are three broad areas of specialist operation:

(1)   marketing (including design and estimating);
(2)   manufacture and distribution; and
(3)   installation (including commissioning).

The feedback to each of these must be in a form such that the reasons for any failure to meet planned objectives may be identified and analysed. In some cases it may be possible to modify a component, a procedure, or a form of organization in such a way as to correct for a deviation from plan within the duration of the contract. In other cases the lesson is one to be applied only in the future. This, too, is valuable: the adaptability and flexibility of a firm in relation to its market can be vital to its prosperity. The identification of overspending may not indicate its cause, and thus each significant instance calls for an explanation. In the normal course of events there are cash-flow fluctuations, and within the course of a contract some of these will be self-correcting. A system therefore needs a set of rules defining warning and danger limits and corresponding forms of action.

The essence of a control system will lie in the selection of cost centres, and these should reflect the stages of the process from design to commissioning. Expenditure during the defects-liability period is mainly an erosion of profit. Suppose, for instance, that in manufacturing there are stages represented by

(1)   materials procurement, storage and supply;
(2)   machine-shop processes;
(3)   assembly-shop processes;
(4)   finishing-shop processes;
(5)   packing and distribution.

Then these will be the prime cost centres. Subcentres may be necessary for the individual manager to trace the sources of overspending to parts of a process. It is possible that this level of control is best operated and maintained separately from the main cost-accounting system.

The proliferation of cost centres must increase the problems of allocation and, once errors of allocation creep in, seeking out and correcting such errors may prove a major impediment to the analysis of sources of loss.

From the tender sum, the revised estimate and the contract programme agreed with the main contractor a budget is prepared. A sum is thus allocated to each cost centre. In some cases, as for design, it may be some percentage of the tender sum, while in others, as for manufacturing, it may incorporate allocations to the factors of production based on detailed estimates of materials cost and wastage, labour productivity, energy consumption and overheads.

Provided the cost centre codes that are entered on to documents appear consistently at all stages of the contract then all else is a matter of certifying the documents and processing. Clearly data cannot be retrieved in more detail than is put into the system but, once retrieved, the data may be presented in many forms. Mechanical data processing, as well as providing a saving in time, enables reports to be made in a variety of forms, so as to meet the needs of estimators, planning engineers, managers, etc.

It is clear, however, that any such structure must be raised on factual input. It will probably be necessary to develop a job-card system that instructs defined groups of operatives on site to go to some place, with listed materials and tools, and carry out a quantity of specified work in a given time. The actual stores consumed and hours worked should then be reported on returning the card, the document serving also as a check on timesheet entries and stores issued.

Where a programme is prepared, with activities listed and coded, the job card may carry both programme and cost references. An advantage of this system would be that differences of cost between similarly coded items on different contract could be traced back to method, manning and stores consumed and the variation explained. In fact, as discussed later in relation to civil engineering, such proposals tend to excessive complexity in coding and allocation. If authenticated data are incorporated into a computer data bank, the mean and standard deviation of such data may be retrieved, on demand, for the benefit of estimators and planners. In this way an element of probability is introduced into forecasting.

Thus we have a combination of factory-type control systems, which compare the delivered cost and value of equipment, and site-control systems based on job cards, which permit the aggregation and analysis of installation costs. As the firm is competing on a performance and cost basis, aspects of design that create site costs, and any site installation requirements that incur costs are of importance. Accordingly, there is a case for coding the work in such a way that its elements are differentiated in terms of both factory and site. Factory costs become items of site-materials cost and the comparison of unit costs on different sites may be of value to designers. It would seem that such systems can contribute not only to the competitive performance of a contractor but also to the economic acceptability of his designers' product.

Recent Cost-Control Developments in Civil Engineering

The Civil Engineering Standard Method of Measurement (C.E.S.M.M) has now completed its development into a bill form that relates its items and quantities more closely to the manner in which construction costs accrue. In U. K. terms it is appropriate, even inevitable, that such a reform should have appeared first in this part of construction. Engineers at different times may be responsible for design, measurement or the construction itself. They have no vested interest in procedures associated with one or the other. In building, the surveying profession arose from the exclusiveness of architects, who excluded both surveyors and contractors from their professional company.

It is necessary also to make clear the distinction between surveyors in private practice and those acting within a contractor's organisation. The current reluctance of the I.Q.S. to form a single learned society with the R.I.C.S. prolongs the sectionalisation of interests. Private practices exist largely to provide a service to clients. They are concerned with investment and return, with advice to designers, and the initiation of documents primarily for contractor selection but later for project control. Their procedures are based on the work as it is intended to be completed on site. On the other hand those who work for a contractor take up their responsibilities when there is a a successful outcome from the estimator's pricing of contract documents. They do not initiate or promote a specific form of contract but merely learn to adapt their procedures to those forms on which their firm tenders. They are concerned with the processes of marketing, in particular tendering and budgeting, and thus with the financial outcomes and control of contracts. Entitlements under the terms of contract become an important part of their expertise. They are required to concern themselves with work in place, but cannot avoid the need of reconciling such data with the costs associated with its construction and the resources required. In reconciling such disparate data they acquire an appreciation of price and cost that is not directly available to a quantity surveyor in private practice.

Barnes (1977a) writing about the C.E.S.M.M., suggests that the bill of quantities should 'comprise a list of carefully described parameters on which the *cost of work* to be done can be expected to depend' (our emphasis). Items in a bill represent a description of building work for *pricing*. Each is an offer; the more the work description departs from method, the more this offer requires judgement bearing in mind contractual tactics and risk. Barnes goes on to point out the inadequacy of quantity as the sole cost-significant variable to be priced. The incidence of a variation will demonstrate that time, access, sequence and equipment differ from those which an estimator might have envisaged.

The nearer that a cost model comes to actuality, the less room there is for disagreement about valuations and variations. There is a narrowing of the disparity between the cost feedback of the contractor and the price feedback of the client's quantity surveyor. The quality of advice to the industry's present clients must then be less satisfactory than it might be. This is a gap which the C.E.S.M.M. seeks to reduce.

Under J.C.T. conditions of contract one expects a bill in which the item description and quantity are specific. An item in a bill drawn up to conform to C.E.S.M.M. may content itself with a description in the form of a reference to a specific drawing and clause in the specification. In the billing under the J.C.T. conditions the private quantity surveyor accepts responsibility for descriptions based sometimes on less than complete information. This is no doubt appreciated by contractors who are presumably not expected to have the interpretative expertise of civil engineers. The part played by civil-engineering drawings and specifications is a facilitating factor in recent revision.

Civil-engineering bills divide the work into sections identified alphabetically, each subdivided according to three selected parameters out of the many variables that might influence cost. Integers 1 to 8 are allocated to specific characteristics of each, such as stated ranges of pipe size or types of excavation (dredging, cuttings, foundations, etc.) while 9 is available for any unlisted classification. A code consisting of a letter and three integers thus offers 24 headings each with over 500 subclassifications by which to tag any bill item. It is not comprehensive: earthworks, for example, which are classified by type, material and method of disposal, might equally be influenced by weather, depth, access and many other variables that the coding ignores. To include all the relevant variables would produce an unwieldy code and such a distribution of stored data that many elements would be statistically unsatisfactory. The system as it stands is a practical proposal that can be utilised as a vehicle for the consistent coding of data input within and between contracts: it may not be the best or the ultimate but it is a workable solution to a difficult problem.

In the context of this book it provides a data framework within which to discuss cost control systems that are more effective and theoretically more satisfying than those which practice has imposed hitherto.

It is not necessary to present the layout of appropriate forms, since the design of these follows unswervingly. Each bill item can be coded (Barnes, 1977b). Each document concerned with resources, timesheet or invoice can be coded directly to a bill item or work section or, in the instance of some bulk supplies, to a suspense-account code for later distribution. Each such document enters the accounting system and can thus be coded, or apportioned between codes, and classified according to the factor of production—labour, materials, plant or overheads—and a chronological list results. At predetermined intervals, daily or weekly, a list of active code numbers can be the vehicle for items to be selected, aggregated and totalled. The outcome is a series of code totals, and of totals by factors of production. The grand total is the invoiced cost to date.

Figure 8.6 is a diagram of the flow of information through a cost-control system of the type envisaged. Figure 8.7 illustrates the form in which original entries may be treated, and the form of summary sheet that could be used to bring together at intervals the cost situation for each cost centre. Figure 8.8 suggests a form in which the contract status might be reported.

Using such a system, it becomes possible to identify cost centres that indicate a level of achievement markedly different from that forecast, and to locate the source of the deviation at the level of the factors of production.

From the bill, standards relating to code totals are available. The combination of progress reports and recorded costs should indicate those codes against which overspending appears to be occurring. The factor(s) of production concerned can be studied and compared with labour forecasts, purchase documents, plant specification and output, etc. The process is one which the computer can handle expeditiously—and indeed with discrimination if so programmed. Strict conditions of statistical significance can be placed upon reports of deviation from plan, and warning and danger limits can be specified and observed.

Of course there are snags. The framework exists but the reality lies beyond a forest of provisos and procedural decisions. Many have been explored in earlier discussions. The crucial ones are those ensuring that accounting dates and data

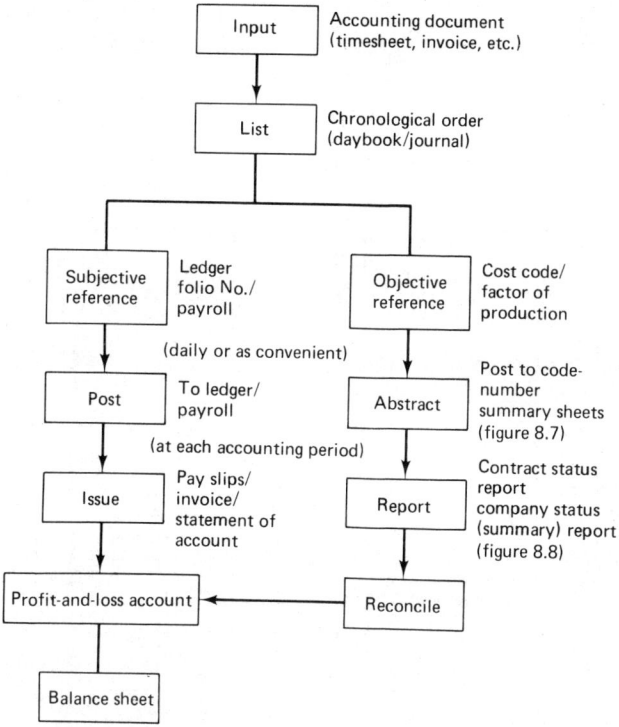

Figure 8.6 Diagram of cost control procedures

are reconciled. If work is valued then resources employed must all appear in costs even if invoices are awaited and the sums concerned require later adjustment. If reports are delayed until accounting documents are processed then the control effectiveness of the system is undermined. Certainly computerisation can hardly be justified unless both control and feedback are available services.

Should such a system be developed, it follows that a planner or estimator could call up data by work classification (code number), either as a total or unit cost, or by its subdivision by factors of production. This data could be in the form of a mean value, a standard deviation, and a correction to a base date. Such information is directly derived and within the capacity of simple computational aids. Control requires an input of standards against which to compare recorded values. However, the target figures in terms of work classification and factors of production should be made subject to review and up dating as a matter of routine.

It would be necessary to record explanatory information about contract or site conditions that give rise to values departing by (say) more than one standard deviation from the mean of any significant sample of data. The system could thus prompt an explanation in anticipation of need. An estimator or planner could then measure the circumstances of his site against factors that in the past have led to extreme values and decide what values he should adopt in relation to the recorded mean.

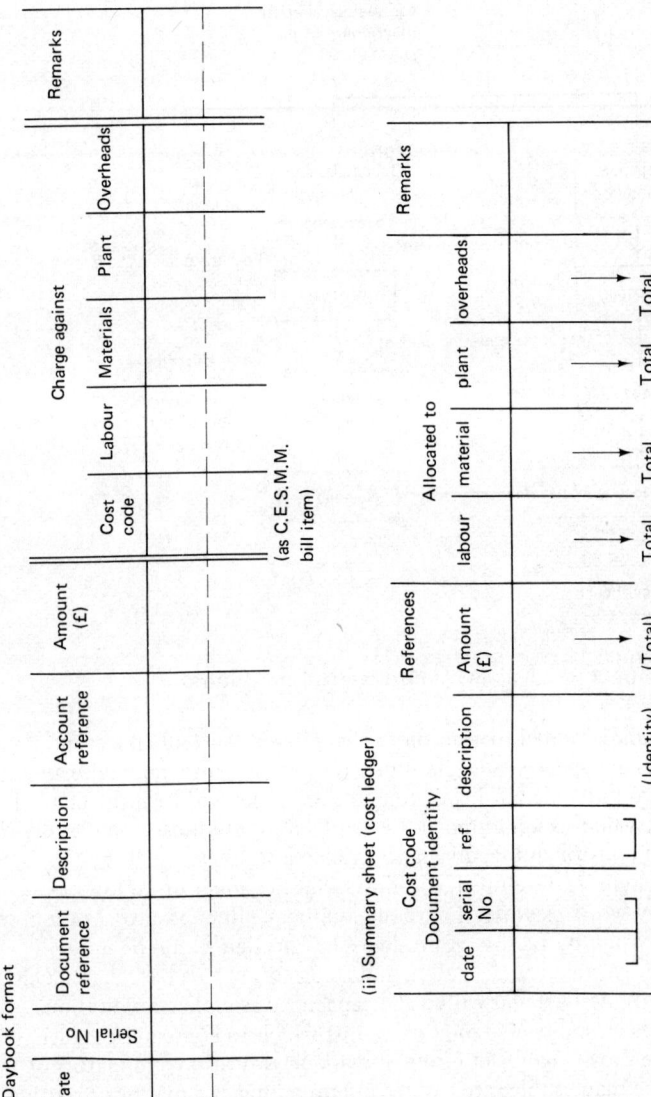

Figure 8.7   Extracts from daybook and cost ledger. Note that all details for posting and reference are included on one line.

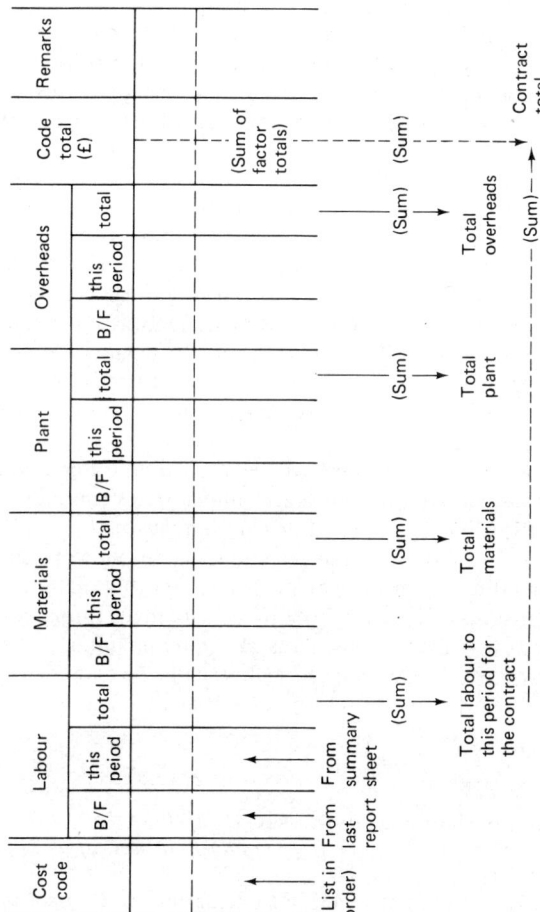

Figure 8.8   Contract cost report. Note that remarks may be expanded to include, for example, percentage completion, budget cost and incident references (weather, breakdown, lack of information, variation order No., etc.).

For most of the items in a bill it might be sufficient to take comfort from Pareto and retrieve only the mean value, corrected for the period beyond the base date, but otherwise entered as a rate without amendment. Indeed computer estimation might become an interactive process between the estimator and his data bank.

This is probably an appropriate place to discuss an ideal system. There is clearly no such thing as an ideal system except in a limited field. The building contract cannot adopt civil engineering work sections, and thus a building and civil engineering contractor cannot have a single system. Complexity leads to allocation problems, and unreliable input is corrosive to effectiveness. Simplicity and coherence demand some form of compromise and there is a risk that a significant factor will be ignored at some time. One is led to a concept of the system based on some divisional organisation, with tactical control reserved for site control systems.

There are, however, civil engineering projects of such scale and complexity that, while the various participating firms might well devise effective systems for themselves, the resulting aggregate would be too complex for the client to articulate at his level. This is serious only if such projects could be repeated without significant change in the future. If each is the product of a single cost–benefit exercise or derives from a decision based on investment analysis, the exercise must depend, as is the case at present, on the quotations of participants.

We hope that civil engineers have not ploughed thus far through our book only to find that they are on the brink of new developments that are not fully explored. The C.E.S.M.M. is relatively new and contracts based on it are hardly likely to be in progress. The illustrations presented so far have been based on observations of practice, because too many books have speculated unprofitably, and the basic system of coding, classification by factors of production, abstracting and reporting that is described is a working and successful system based on the work classifications of past standard methods of measurement. The form of tabulation described adapts well to computerisation. However, only by development into areas of estimating feedback and cost advice on the basis of *common* coding procedure (now offered by the current C.E.S.M.M.), can such systems be extended to afford a service that is greater than the sum of its parts; for that we must wait.

References

Barnes, M., *Measurement in Contract Control* (I.C.E., 1977a).
Barnes, M., *Examples of the Civil Engineering Standard Method of Measurement* (I.C.E., 1977b).
Kelsey, K. J., 'Financial Control in Mechanical Contracting', in *Control of Engineering Projects,* ed. S. H. Wearne (Arnold, London, 1974), chapter 5.

9 Computers in Construction

Computers appear to be grossly underutilised in construction. They are becoming less expensive all the time. While there is no doubt about their capacity to handle data and there is no denying the need for information, the industry, as a whole, has been unable or unwilling to regulate its structure and procedures so that this capacity may be exploited to the full.

Businessmen have been bound in many cases by established procedures. They have tended to maintain procedures instead of developing them into more effective aids to decision-making. This might involve considerable investment and there is always the risk that some industry-wide reform would render the results obsolete.

For twenty years or so, large computer firms have had software packages that facilitate planning, resources levelling and program updating. They can cope with variety in the manner in which resources are defined and offer choice in exercising limits in terms of time, resources or their functions (and the aggregated effect of resources and time is readily converted to cost) when programs are updated. Construction firms have probably invested thousands of pounds in their own systems. They all see the importance of detailed and realistic standards by which to monitor performance, and recognise the need to react in the event of serious deviations in performance from plan. Nevertheless the extension of computer usage has not proceeded at the pace that might have been expected.

If the cost of setting up the system, monitoring procedures and reporting is great, the perceived savings or reduction of risk must cover it. It follows that the objectives of the system must be clearly understood, articulated and evaluated before the capacity of the computer can be brought to bear most effectively.

There are now computer services that prepare software packages for machines in a specific range and offer them to industry as single services—stock control, payroll, etc. Thus, subsequent reports relating to finance, plant utilisation, stock control, and other such aspects of construction activity are offered as data-processing services in competition with orthodox manual methods.

The computer firms see at once that, given the input to establish the service that they offer, they can sort, sift and reinterpret it in a number of ways to expand the range of information output. Offers of equipment incorporate software refinements of many kinds even if, in many cases, demonstrations of such outputs are the vehicle for computer sales rather than computer service.

Robinson's research at Salford University into the specific application of computers in construction is concerned with the practical expression of skills and capabilities that are required by industry. We are indebted to him for some of the general notes and observations that follow.

At a conference organized by the C.I.R.I.A. information liaison group the role of an information system was stated to be

(1)   to classify information in categories that users need;
(2)   to identify resources so that the flow of information does not have to be encumbered with long and significant descriptions and class indicators;
(3)   to describe the resources used in construction, giving data of direct interest to all participants;
(4)   to describe projects especially in terms of the geometric form and position of commodities;
(5)   to foster the development of procedures by agreed conventions including a preferred vocabulary;
(6)   to support information flow and achieve economy—roles that pervade the others, and include the multiple use of data and standard details, specifications, etc.

The first observation arising from this role definition is that the first five items *precede* any consideration of data processing, whether by computer or not. The second is that multiple use data, which are a feature of computerised data processing, depend upon the compatibility of input data and the various forms of output. Therefore, conventions based on current practice must be revised and made compatible *before* adoption.

Job costing systems depend on someone making the decisions inherent in data coding. Such codes may, at some stage of financial accounting, be required to identify

(1)   the business unit to which the account pertains—the divisions, region, or subsidiary concerned;
(2)   the site or contract;
(3)   the job or cost centre for which specific resources are intended or to which they are to be allocated;
(4)   the nature of the expense (labour, materials, etc.).

Few companies would need more than the ten options that are offered by a single-digit numerical code in order to satisfy the range of (1), more than the thousand offered by a three-digit code for (2) and more than a single digit again for (4). However, even in a telephone number a seven-digit group is hard enough to memorise. We would be asking site clerks and foremen to become familiar with, and enter onto time sheets and requisitions, as many code numbers as there are active cost centres associated with the work for which they are responsible. It must make the reliability of code allocation something of a problem.

Building performance is influenced by ground and climatic conditions, height and exposure, workspace congestion, continuity of work and many other variables. If therefore the effect of such factors is to be enumerated and stored for further reference, additional subcoding cannot be avoided.

Codes issued for a specific job may be few, but if there is to be a feedback of information to estimators and planners then the performance of one job must be compared at some stage with that of others, and there is an argument for a standard coding system within a firm. This would have to provide for a wider range of activities than those of a single job.

The veracity of the input data, including coding, is vital to the effectiveness of a computer-based system. Once a process of query and reconciliation stands between a deviation from a plan and the action to rectify it, delays eat into system effectiveness. Not only must the relationship between activities and cost codes be readily seen, but the selection and entry of the code has to be as foolproof as possible.

It is clear that cost codes based on 'in-place' work, as in the items of a trade bill, introduce complications for the initiator of cost data. Operational coding might simplify the decision as to which cost centres correspond to an item of account. Such a system should also be more readily understood by workface supervisors, who, in general, dislike administrative procedures, and become very unsettled if responsibility for clerical error is pressed on them.

Trade bill based data afford a direct link between estimating procedures and the financial performance of a single contract. The financial status, however, is tied to a monthly cycle, whereas site tactics are a weekly affair, if not a matter of hour-to-hour and day-to-day decision-making. Looked at from the point of view of control, therefore, the period of the feedback cycle is too long.

Day-to-day activities centre on resources, time and output. Production targets are set by reference to some cost and value, and performance is thus set at a quantity with implications as to quality and resources (inspection standards, man and machine hours, power and materials wastage). Cost is a retrospective judgement. If the statement of cost awaits even the submission, let alone the payment of accounts, it may appear only some weeks after the event. Labour cost, materials cost or plant cost, taken separately, can be misleading: for instance, they may fail to show advantageous changes of method. The observation of performance must be related to a measurement of physical progress. By comparing man and plant hours with predetermined targets and materials cost and wastage, the chance that the deviation between financial and physical performance will go uncorrected is reduced. To extend the process to cost comparisons, so that financial status is reported rapidly in the form of computer print-out, calls for more planning, investment and training within the organisation than is immediately obvious. Only then can the machine help.

Construction managers will be aware that any tactical plan is in need of frequent review and revision. Progress control based on (say) network analysis can only be sensitive to adjustment of tactics by continuous updating. The precedence diagram, which simply details strategy, affords a simple basis for codes. Tactical planning, based on subnets, may then take place as a separate site exercise and be reflected in subcodes only. If the site has its own minicomputer then some subdivision of strategic and tactical control is possible. Only the broad activities on different jobs need attract the same codes. Subcodes for the computer analysis of site progress need not be standardised, and only a summary in a standard format need be passed onward to the firm's data-processing procedures.

Timesheets are the basic input for payroll purposes and if these are coded by activity, as we have been considering, then the labour costs have to be converted to bill-item format before being included in cost-value comparisons. This suggests that perhaps the hope of one great integrated data system can only be realised if the bill format is based on activities. Attempts, thus far, to take this idea to its logical conclusion indicate a multiplicity of entries. Some work, otherwise appearing as a single item, must appear in a number of places to account for peculiarities of sequence or location. Also, items distributed by phase and sequence may have to be brought together again for subcontractor quotation purposes. Once again such items should presumably be subcoded and only their aggregate be reported upward in a specified standard form.

The alternative offered by the C.E.S.M.M. is to restrict coding to areas of construction activity identified according to three selected variables, whatever number may, in fact, be seen to influence performance. Any item falling within the general area of civil engineering construction should then be capable of identification with a code comprising a letter (or two digits) and three further digits. These should apply to similar work on that or any other site. It is immediately manageable within its context and, if not comprehensive, is practical.

Data for the use of estimators and planners must, or should, include subcode information reflecting site and external factors that have affected cost in the past experience of the firm. Perhaps on job completion a statement reconciling site costs and headquarters costs should be prepared as part of the final account procedure so that, having allowed for factors arising from site and contract variations, cost data may be stored for future use. The value of explanations goes beyond that of immediate clarification, since they provide information about ranges of performance and the factors relating to variations between different sites and situations.

Thus, the indications are that, outside firms with narrow marketing objectives (for example, specialising in subtrades work on the one hand or say housing or single-storey factory building on the other), the idea of a viable integrated data-processing system depends upon preparatory standardisation. A standard method of measurement for building that is more closely related to construction method and a bill format reflecting such a method might bring cost and price into a better relationship. It might permit cost centres to be related to bill items on the one hand and aggregates of related activities on the other.

Once the conditions are established there is no doubt that the mechanical capability to process, sort, analyse and report can be put to use for the benefit of all within, and served by, the industry.

In researching into computer applications in construction Tong (1977) found little evidence of radical developments since the survey by Urwick Dynamics Ltd (1974), which indicated that systems in use were predominantly concerned with financial rather than managerial accounting. Among larger firms there was no lack of investment, but equally no trend of activity toward a common database permitting better utilisation of data by feedback from costing to planning and estimating. Systems for each function tended to be self-contained.

Bureaux apparently offer a cost model package, which is designed to facilitate resources planning and allocation on site. One company has a standard package permitting the site manager whose site is large enough to justify the issue of a mini-computer to initiate and process his own cost analysis, budget comparison and forecasts.

The Civil Service has a Standing Committee on computing and data coordination, which stems from a working party set up in 1966. After 10 years it apparently offered little but an exhortation that steps be taken to improve communications in the industry, which is where the industry left things when it withdrew its support from the research project by the Tavistock Institute of Human Relations some 11 years previously.

There is no denying the power and potential of computers and, with the steady development of minicomputers, their convenience and flexibility. The great deal of money that has been invested in studies thus far has resulted in little improvement to the over-all service offered to the public by the industry. At the foundation of any such service lies a proper record of information that can only be gained at the workface of the industry. Until output and resources are related, there is nowhere to go.

The Equipment Available

The computer can store vast amounts of information and sift and sort it very rapidly. This enables its use to be extended from accountancy to that of general management, given the instructions (programs) to process an appropriate input of data.

The following facilities are available for first-time users.

Visible-record Computers (V.R.C.)

These have developed from conventional account machines. They cost from £5000 in 1976, and prices have fallen since. Programs suitable for most basic accounting procedures are provided. Information is often stored on magnetic strips. The equipment is relatively simple and easy to use. In the past there has been only a limited capacity for sorting information automatically or referring to information if it was available only in a random order, but such limitations are becoming fewer.

The Minicomputer

The potential and flexibility of the minicomputer have led to its introduction in companies at site and office level. No special environmental control is needed, and such computers operate from a 13-amp plug. In 1976 the cost was in the tens of thousands of pounds but installations have become more complex, more effective and very much cheaper since then (see p. 141). With the introduction of microcoded functionality a number of virtual memories has extended the data-storage and data-processing capacity. By the introduction of a printer or a video display unit interactive processing became possible.

Computer Bureaux

Access to a large main-firm system serviced by a complex library of software and trained and specialised computer staff can be covered by payment on a time rate. This type of service allows a contractor to gain experience of the problems and benefits of mechanical data processing without a heavy initial investment. Some may well then choose to centre their processing around such services.

Batch Bureau Services

This form of service makes maximum use of computer time because the input is arranged in the optimum sequence to suit the nature of the data in the memory.

Properly prepared data must be submitted for processing by means of a data-delivery service by a contracted time. The average turnround time is 24 to 48 h at a price ranging upward from £20 per computer hour. Extra costs arise if demand includes data storage, priority runs, punching, data delivery and collection.

On-line Bureau Services

At present, three types of on-line service are available: remote batch entry, remote job entry, and interactive computing.

In *remote batch entry* (R.B.E.) the user submits his program via a terminal in his premises to the central computing system at some other location via the G.P.O. Datel Telephone Service. The data are received at the central computer, stored for later processing in batch mode and, after processing, are transferred back to the terminal.

Remote job entry (R.J.E.) is similar to remote batch entry except that the work is normally submitted to the processor while you wait. In some cases the user is allowed a limited amount of interactive editing and validation.

In *interactive computing*, the program is compiled and executed on a statement-by-statement basis, which does not optimise the central processor's time. Most bureaux offer services centred round specific systems relating to accounts, payroll, network anaylsis, etc.

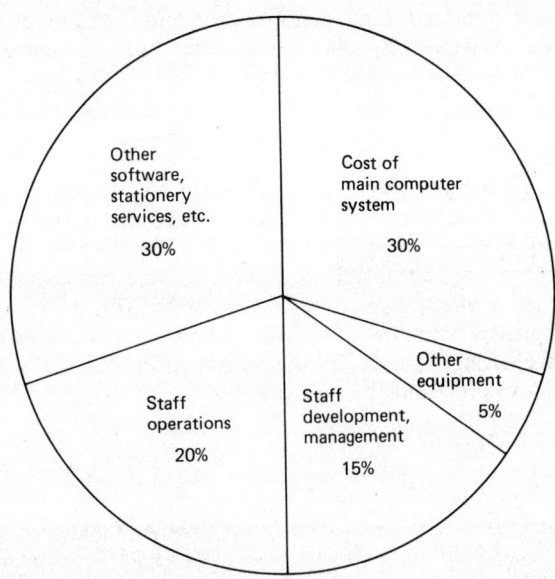

Figure 9.1   Distribution of computer costs

In-house Computer

The investment in staff and equipment calls for a high and uniform workload in order to justify investment. It also calls for a level of initiative and imagination that will exploit the capabilities of the system to promote the firm's efficiency.

The typical cost distribution is shown in figure 9.1.

Programmable Prompting Calculators

These are being developed as a half-way stage from electronic calculators to mini-computers. They cost as little as £2000 in 1977 and vary in range and power according to cost. Much routine accountancy and analysis is within their capacity and they have a limited printout function.

In his studies Robinson prepared a number of decision charts, which readers involved in the consideration of computer installations may care to peruse.

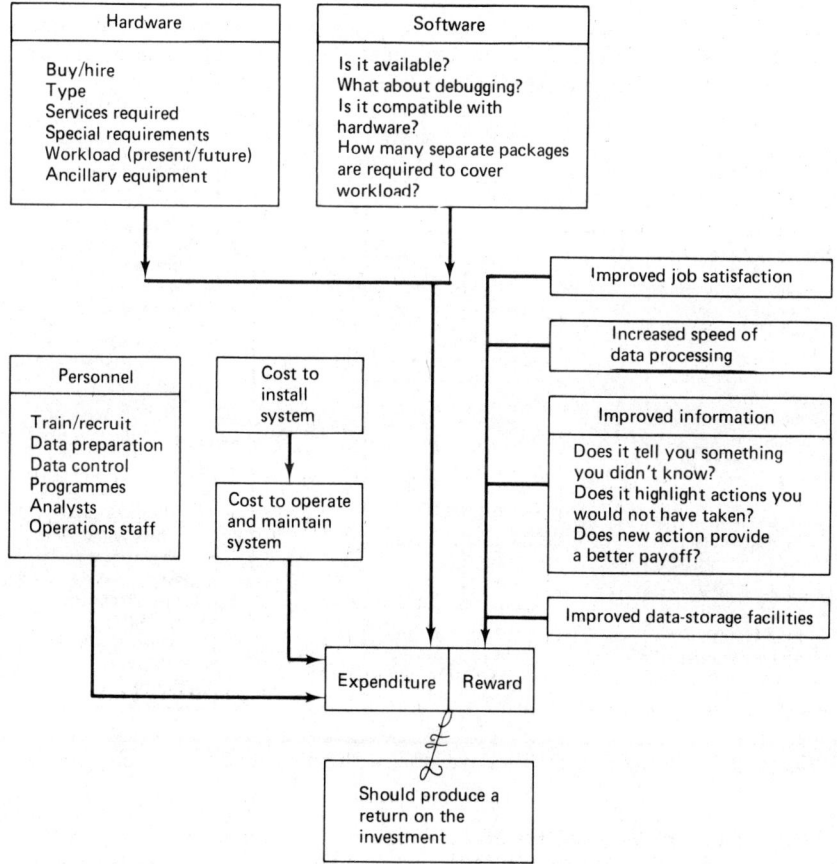

Figure 9.2 Decision areas for computer selection

The range of decisions that must be considered by a firm in selecting one or other of the above options is shown in figure 9.2.

Once access has been gained to computing facilities, by one of the above means, the firm's systems analysts (or those of a bureau) can set up a system for a particular need. Packages are offered for

(1)   the calculation of wages and salaries;
(2)   labour costing;
(3)   ledger account;
(4)   purchase analysis;
(5)   materials transactions;
(6)   plant costing;
(7)   network analysis;
(8)   contract costing, etc.

The descending order represents one that is perhaps appropriate to firms moving into the field. A programme for budgetary control, for instance, calls for input from other options and for some time at least may be processed manually since it is required relatively infrequently. An example of a range of information gained from a single set of data is offered in figure 9.3.

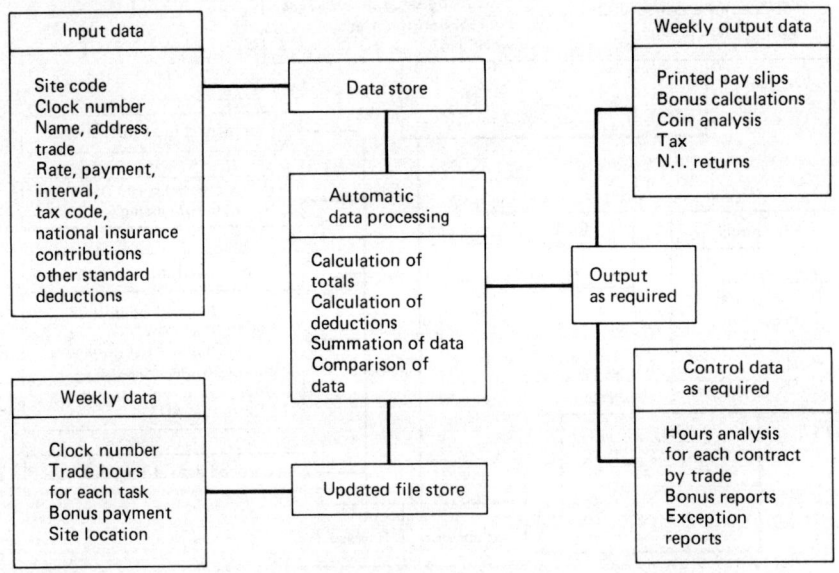

Figure 9.3   Outline of facilities available with an automatic payroll system

The computer is also capable of simulating an action or series of actions so that some indication of the payoff from the decision may be ascertained before any commitment is made to a particular strategy. Examples are to be found in the application of network analysis.

Network Analysis (P.E.R.T.)

Network analysis programs are available for initial contract planning and for contract progress control. They are designed so that available resources may be optimised within the cost and time restraints. Figure 9.4 illustrates such a system. Networks have proved to be of more use in preparing programs than in expressing them, except in those rare situations when time is of the essence and resources can be deployed on demand. They do nevertheless permit 'crash programming' decisions to be simulated and tested. Such exercises call for additional inputs relating to cost and benefit.

A network is concerned with sequence, and one sequence of activities may be selected from a number of alternatives at certain points. If that which is selected fails, then the manager may have alternatives that are not contained in the net-work: it does not set out to cover all possible routes to an object. Too detailed a network is open to frequent revision, which may be expensive; too crude a net-work omits essential detail.

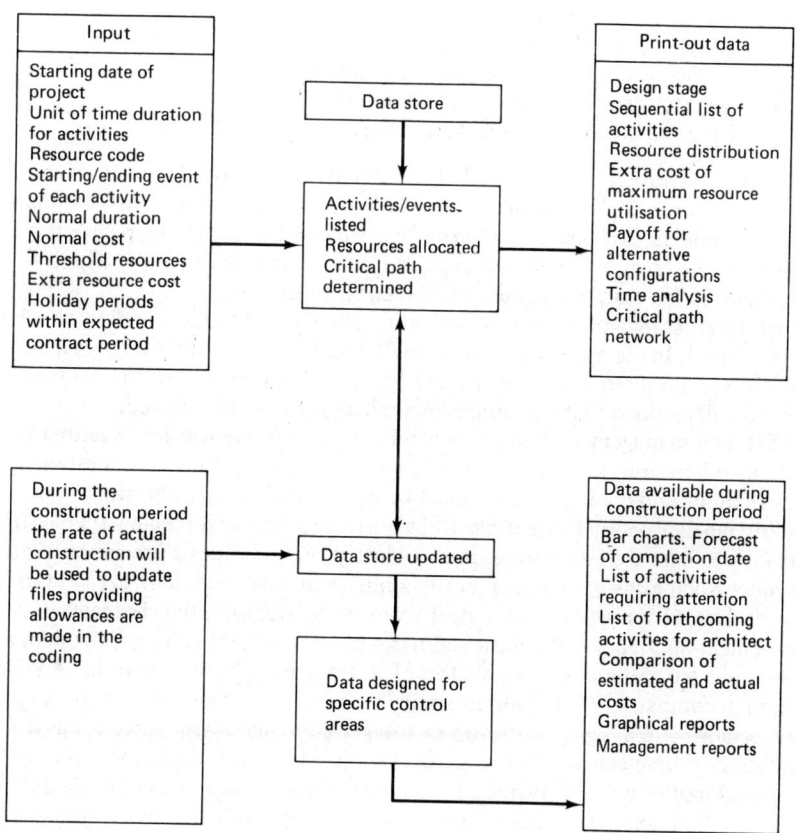

Input		Print-out data
Starting date of project Unit of time duration for activities Resource code Starting/ending event of each activity Normal duration Normal cost Threshold resources Extra resource cost Holiday periods within expected contract period	Data store Activities/events. listed Resources allocated Critical path determined	Design stage Sequential list of activities Resource distribution Extra cost of maximum resource utilisation Payoff for alternative configurations Time analysis Critical path network
During the construction period the rate of actual construction will be used to update files providing allowances are made in the coding	Data store updated Data designed for specific control areas	Data available during construction period Bar charts. Forecast of completion date List of activities requiring attention List of forthcoming activities for architect Comparison of estimated and actual costs Graphical reports Management reports

Figure 9.4   Outline of facilities available for network analysis

The Building Research Establishment has been concerned with problems of activity definition. In order to store and recover data for reference, they must be measured consistently. If they are then to be processed so as to answer questions put by designers (about the cost of elements of a building) or by estimators (about the cost of work in place) they must again be measured in suitable terms. In the event of some satisfactory solution to such intractable problems there would be basic units of information round which to design a coherent system of record and feedback.

Cash Flow Forecasting

Professor E. G. Trimble, at Loughborough University of Technology, has some years' experience of programs to forecast a firm's cash requirements each quarter from

(1)   the duration of existing and proposed projects;
(2)   project value estimates;
(3)   cost liability estimates;
(4)   payment delays for various categories of cost;
(5)   retention percentage and maximum value;
(6)   delays between valuations and payment.

This form of information has already been discussed. It may allow a contractor to make organisational decisions on the basis of possible future events, comparing different strategies to meet best the organisation's goals. Being in a position to renegotiate the terms of loans and appraise the alternative courses by which to gain resources for work ahead has self-evident benefits.

Such forecasting and control are valuable, and are as good as the data on which they are based. Inadequacies of data show themselves more when there is need for detail. It is when reasons for unexpected features in the output of the control system are demanded that the underlying reliability of data is tested.

Whether a management budgeting team, a planning engineer or an estimator needs information to solve some specific and important but limited question, the data input and coding systems must be comprehensive and the stored data properly labelled. Sometimes it has to be corrected for unavoidable variables or reduced to a base date and value. In an industry that provides a service rather than a product, such a system has to identify similar circumstances in order to retrieve relevant data. Circumstances may be influenced by weather, the character of management and labour, the local and national economy, the design, the demand on the industry and many other factors. The storage problem is obvious. A large Australian company offering services ranging from consultancy to contracting, and specialising in a highly professional integrated management service, has a computerised financial and cost control system, which, it claims, does most of the things required of an ideal system. It converts all input data to a common database and the system is said to produce daily, weekly or monthly details of project costs, debtors, creditors, liquidity and general financial control. We are indebted to A. C. Sidwell for information on the subject and would quote his belief that the scheme was made possible because the 'comprehensive design and construction service

[was] not hidebound by the requirement to produce a detailed bill of quantities'.

Two trends are apparent. There is a body of increasingly numerate managers. The proportion is appreciably lower in building than in civil engineering, however. There is evidence that definition of work sections is possible in the civil-engineering sector of construction, and recognition of the possibilities arising from such standardisation is making itself known to those facing similar problems in building. The extension of university and polytechnic schools of surveying, a more numerate approach in schools of architecture and some commitment by industry to mid-career training for its corps of managers may well provide the spur to a wider adoption of computer methods.

Microcomputers/Microprocessors

These are small semi-portable systems, capable of carrying out all the fundamental routines of a larger computer and having from 4k to 48k random access and/or read only memory. The basic desk-top VDU terminal can be extended to provide limited hard copy and floppy disc storage if required. They provide a powerful tool for single-purpose or a group of predetermined processes; many new application fields, with the necessary software, are currently being developed.

References

Tong, M. K., *The Use of Computers in Construction,* M. Sc. Dissertation (University of Aston, Birmingham, 1977).

Urwick Dynamics Ltd, *A Survey of Computers in the Construction Industry* (1974).

10   Business Decisions

The object of financial control, apart from attempting to anticipate and counter disadvantgeous changes of business fortune, is to help to make the best use of financial resources. The board of directors is responsible to the shareholders for the conduct of the business. It is frequently faced with choices between alternative courses of action, and many of them have financial implications. Whether it is a matter of investment or a marketing choice these may be indissolubly mixed with factors arising from considerations of personnel or technology. Individual directors must have some appreciation of all the factors, even if there are some in which they are expert. In addition the board of a modern company is served by extensive data-processing and information services, and the proper interpretation of reports is a growing responsibility. Indeed in accepting board responsibility the necessity for a wider range of evaluation techniques impresses itself. It becomes necessary to be alive to inflexions of meaning in considering the reports that reach the board.

The firm itself figures in other people's decisions and thus the firm's presentation of information about its capacity and performances is also important.

It may be useful in the first place to express the elements of business finance in as concise a form as possible.

A firm invests in *fixed assets* (I_f) of accommodation, plant, equipment, transport and so on in order to prosecute its business. It gains *working capital* (I_w) to finance day-to-day operations. It undertakes auxiliary investment to make the best use of temporary surpluses and to have assets that are rapidly convertible to cash (I_a). The total *risk capital* (I_c) is the sum of these. It requires a return in profits, interest or dividends, which are extracted from the flow of money through the firm in increments as the work proceeds. Most of the income of the firm is recirculated to meet costs and expenses. What is often a delicate balance between inputs and outputs survives only by grace of the confidence of employees, suppliers, subcontractors and clients. A flight of confidence impresses on the firm the need to support and justify its every move, and few are so well managed that this can be taken as read.

Manufacturing or processing costs (C_m) have a fixed element (C_f), which affords the facility, and variable one (C_v) arising from inputs of labour, materials and energy according to the throughput of work. Note that C_v is not necessarily *uniformly* variable, often being a step function; C_f has two elements—C_{f1}, the fixed costs of production, and C_{f2}, the fixed costs of organisation and equipment, marketing and distribution.

If then we denote *gross profit* by G and *sales income* by S

$$G = S - (C_{f1} + C_v)$$

details of which are gained from the trading account (not necessarily published), whereas *net profit* (N) is derived by deducting C_{f2} and depreciation from G. Depreciation is a function of I_f—say kI_f

$$N = G - (C_{f2} + kI_f)$$

and by substituting for G

$$N = S - (C_m + kI_f)$$

The data for the former expression appear in the profit-and-loss-account; these are the data most often used.

The rate of depreciation is not a single value, but varies according to the nature of fixed asset and the acceptability of the rate to the Inland Revenue service.

Taxation is subject to arbitrary rules of imposition. If it were to be levied on gross profit then it would appear in the profit-and-loss account and be deducted to arrive at the net profit figure. Where, as in the United Kingdom, it is levied on net profit, which is a figure to be gained from the audited accounts published under company law, it appears under current liabilities in the balance sheet. It follows that, in order to arrive at a profit-after-tax figure, we require to know what additions to reserves are shown and the amount of distributed profit. The balance sheet should provide these data. It is of course possible that funds have been taken from reserves to make up an acceptable dividend.

Available data from which we may gain comparative information are as follows:

(1)   The *gross profit* is in itself of little significance but, as a percentage of turnover (usually stated), indicates the trading margin.

(2)   The *net profit* is the profit before tax (in the United Kingdom) appearing in the profit-and-loss account. If expressed as a percentage of turnover and compared with the corresponding figure for the gross profit, it indicates the effect of fixed costs of installations and over-all control.

(3)   The *profit after tax* permits the return against the capital employed to be assessed. The balance sheet permits the deduction of current liabilities from the total of fixed and current assets, giving capital employed. Again both net profit and profit after tax, expressed as a percentage of capital employed, give some reading of financial effectiveness.

These comparisons depend upon a variety of procedures and practice. The manner of valuation of stock in hand and of work in progress can differ between firms. Unrealisable value may be included and the gross profit of the trading account could thus be exaggerated. The value of fixed assets may be the purchase cost less depreciation, which, in times of monetary devaluation, might underestimate the realisable value of buildings and land and the resale value of plant, thus understating the capital employed.

Accounts relate to some specific date. We have seen that, in order to compare statements of account with performance, we have to reconcile one with the other. Entitlements and liabilities that are in process of verification or negotiation have to be brought into account. Published accounts tend to be one-sided and unrecon-

ciled. The auditors ensure that contributory data are based upon properly documented entries but they are not necessarily qualified to dispute the valuation of
stock, work in hand, or certain assets. There are many variables and, by manipulation, some indices may be made to look better than they might. For instance,
to realise assets but delay payment may look better in terms of profit at the
expense of solvency. It becomes necessary, therefore, to analyse accounts for a
number of features, but that is not all.

Procedures and practice vary between firms and thus, unless the policy relating to valuation and depreciation is known, it is not necessarily useful to compare one firm's performance indices with those of another. On the other hand
if a firm's results, prepared in a similar way and recorded over a number of years,
can be represented by trend lines then a valid basis for comparison exists.

Balance Sheet Indices

Liabilities are what the business owes. Among the items will be found

    (1)   capital repayment (to shareholders);
    (2)   loan capital (to sources);
    (3)   reserves (to shareholders);
    (4)   retained profit (to shareholders);
    (5)   current liabilities—creditors, tax, dividends, etc.

Assets are what the business owns. Among the items will be found

    (1)   intangibles, such as goodwill;
    (2)   fixed assets, such as buildings, land, plant;
    (3)   current assets, such as stock, work in hand, debtors, cash.

The shareholder entitlement, or *ownership funds,* appear above.

External liabilities, that is, the repayment of any debentures, loans and outstanding creditor accounts, must be seen to be assured by convertible assets, or
else anxious creditors will take steps to gain payment and threaten the firm's
solvency. Provided this can *just* be done, the firm is solvent but there is no remainder from which to repay shareholders.

The *net worth* of a firm is the difference between its total assets and its external liabilities. Intangible assets are at best estimates, and fixed assets are the
subject of valuation; however, revaluations and undistributed profits account for
much of the book value of reserves which are only realisable by sale of assets.
Undervalued assets depress the reported net worth of the firm. A combination
of undervalued assets and low dividends, leading to a low share price, is an invitation for takeover. On the other hand if the analyst doubts the firm's ability to
cover its ownership funds he may suspect that there will be pressure within the
firm to rectify the position. It is clearly important to pursue the matter so as to
be assured that, for example, delaying payment will not provoke suppliers to hold
back their deliveries. By minimising the investment of resources in its contracts the
firm may spend a great deal of effort in justifying delay rather than promoting
progress.

A firm is *solvent* if it can meet its current liabilities by realising its current
assets. However, creditors may be due for settlement within 30 days, while the

realisation of assets could take longer. Stock and work in progress are often such assets. Usually bridging finance is available, often by an extension of overdraft facilities if the bank manager is satisfied with regard to the firm's financial standing. In the absence of support the firm may have to go into voluntary liquidation to prove its solvency. Should assurance be required, then recoverable debts (which can be sold at a discount), convertible securities (which have a market value), and cash in hand and at the bank can be identified as *liquid assets,* and if these equal current liabilities then no problem exists. Dividing current assets by current liabilities gives the *current ratio,* while dividing liquid assets by current liabilities gives the *quick ratio.* The quick ratio should be unity, or slightly more. If it is much more, funds that could be earning money are idle; and if it is less than unity, there is a threat to the continuity of trading.

In the course of his research at Aston University, Twitty (1977) demonstrated that the factors already discussed in connection with accountancy conventions had tended to give disturbingly low values of the current and quick ratios from construction firms' accounts. He showed that values derived by management accounting procedures appeared to correct the discrepancy and indicated the necessity for caution in forming conclusions on the basis of some data.

Clearly a check on solvency and liquidity should precede consideration of other indices. The purpose of the analysis determines which of the many such indices are relevant. Assuming that we are not concerned with share price and performance, but rather with a firm's financial standing and performance, values might be sought, for instance, for gross profit/turnover (read from the profit and loss account), net profit/capital employed (the latter from the balance sheet), sales/fixed assets, etc. A composite picture is thus built up from which to assess the firm.

Valuations and Comparisons

Money which constitutes the net worth of a firm might have been otherwise employed. If, in a safe investment, it could have been earning some percentage return, then taking into account the relative risk involved some other percentage may be seen to be necessary if the investment is to be justified. In comparing the alternative uses of a firm's money there is a need to consider the criteria very carefully, since the credence to be put upon the outcome of the arithmetic depends upon their validity.

Money is a means to an end, and a financial return on investment may not be that end. Investment in production capacity, for instance, calls for the creation and maintenance of the capacity, and thus the profits must provide not only a financial return but the wherewithal to replace obsolete equipment and to maintain premises. There is a need to make projections of a very speculative nature, but that is often better than failing to take account of future possibilities at all.

The environment in which money is raised and employed is subject to changes of market, which are a part of commercial risk, and also of legislative change, which can, overnight, alter the balance of factors affecting taxation, company law, tenure of ownership and so on. Business decisions can only be made on the best information at the time, and the outcome of a number of possible courses may have to be investigated in order that the risk of being wrong is understood.

It follows that, for instance, the treatment of inflationary trends must be speculative, and a decision may have to be made on the assumption that some rate will not be exceeded. Certainly the existence of inflation has led to a substantial decline in the importance of investments for perpetuity, and almost any agreement now incorporates some updating or renegotiating option. Thus, a combination of short-term measures and high interest rates has changed the approach to valuation.

A calculator with logarithmic functions and memory is needed for calculations on the following pages.

Simple Interest

To repay a loan after some time with simple interest implies that the principal will be returned, together with some percentage per period in interest. If S is the sum returned, then it equals the principal (P) multiplied by $1 + ni$ where n is the number of periods and i the rate of interest expressed as a decimal fraction.

EXAMPLE 10.1

A firm makes £20 000 available to a subsidiary on the understanding that it will be returned after five years with its real value maintained. If, at the end of that period, inflation represents an average of 14 per cent, then

$$S = P(1 + ni)$$
$$= 20\,000\,(1 + 5 \times 0.14)$$
$$= 34\,000$$

Thus the parent company would expect £34 000.

To arrive at an average rate of 14 per cent, the annual rates might have been 17, 16, 15, 12 and 10. If then the subsidiary decided to pay back interest as it arose it would have paid

$$20\,000 \times 0.17 = 3400$$
$$0.16 = 3200$$
$$0.15 = 3000$$
$$0.12 = 2400$$
$$0.1 \;\; = \underline{2000}$$
$$14\,000$$

Adding the principal to this figure again yields £34 000.

Such terms are found where money is deposited on a mortgage loan with (say) a local authority, and periodic interest payments are received. Where interest may be retained and so itself qualify for interest, other conditions apply.

Compound Interest

Where interest accumulates and itself earns, the sum takes the following form

$$S = P(1 + i)^n$$

and our £20 000 over 5 years at 14 per cent per annum would become £38 508.29.

However, taken a year at a time we would have the following amounts

$$20\,000 \times 0.17 = 3400 + 20\,000 = 23\,400$$

$$23\,400 \times 0.16 = 3744 + 23\,400 = 27\,144$$

$$27\,144 \times 0.15 = 4072 + 27\,144 = 31\,216$$

$$31\,216 \times 0.12 = 3746 + 31\,216 = 34\,962$$

$$34\,962 \times 0.1 = 3496 + 34\,962 = 38\,458$$

In this case, adding £38 458 to the principal does *not* give the same result. Thus, in making some projection of future interest significantly different results than were forecast may arise if there are changes that differ from the speculative values used in the calculations. While some rates form part of an agreeement, others are variables, and procedures must recognise that.

When comparing sums of money payable in the future it is necessary to relate them to a single datum. From the compound-interest formula above it follows that

$$P = \frac{S}{(1+i)^n}$$

and the *present worth* of a sum S in n periods at a rate of interest i can be determined.

Again we can accumulate a sum of money after n periods at $i\%$ by making regular fixed payments (R). It follows that after one payment

$$S = R$$

while after two

$$S = R + R(1+i)$$

and after n payments

$$S = R[1 + \ldots + (1+i)^{n-2} + (1+i)^{n-1}]$$

Summing the series

$$S = R\left[\frac{(1+i)^n - 1}{i}\right]$$

that is, we have the *future worth* of a series of payments.

From the above formula we have

$$R = S\left[\frac{i}{(1+i)^n - 1}\right]$$

giving the uniform payments to provide a future sum—the *sinking fund.*

EXAMPLE 10.2

An item of plant is costed at £12 000, to be written off to a scrap value of £1000 over 7 years. However, a replacement will be necessary at the end of that time, and inflation is running at 20 per cent, with a prospect of reduction to 10 per cent in 2 years and to 6 per cent at 5 years and beyond.

The straight-line depreciation of £11 000 over 7 years is £1571 p.a. and this is likely to be the reduction in asset value allowed. Additional funding may thus have to be provided after tax.

Speculating that if projections of inflation rates are realised the annual rates might be 20, 15, 10, 8, 6, 6, 6, we have an harmonic mean of approximately 8.5, and the estimated cost of new plant and salvage value of the old plant in 7 years will be

$$\text{Replacement}-12\,000\,(1 + 0.085)^7 = 21\,242$$

$$\text{Scrap value} \quad - \quad 1000\,(1 + 0.085)^7 = \underline{\quad 1770\quad}$$

$$\text{By subtraction, sinking fund} \quad\quad = 19\,472$$

Money placed on 7-year loan can obtain 11 per cent interest, but with declining rates in inflation it is postulated that not more than 8 per cent can be depended on at the end of a period such as that on which we have been working. Adopt an average of 9.5 per cent

$$\text{Sinking fund payments} = 19\,472 \left[\frac{0.095}{(1.095)^7 - 1} \right]$$

$$= 2084$$

Thus, for an annual transfer to reserves of £2084 some £513 p.a. over and above the likely rate of depreciation will have to be found.

The amount that can be borrowed against periodic repayments R over n periods at i per cent—the present worth of a series of payments contracted against some requirement—can be calculated as follows.

The future worth of a principal obtained on loan is

$$P(1 + i)^n = S$$

From a series of payments

$$S = R \left[\frac{(1 + i)^n - 1}{i} \right]$$

Thus

$$P = R \left[\frac{(1 + i)^n - 1}{i(1 + i)^n} \right]$$

EXAMPLE 10.3

A firm wishes to invest rents of £2400 p.a. over 5 years in a social club for its workers. A brewery offers capital against such payments on loan at a favourable rate of 5 per cent. How much can the firm spend?

$$P = 2400 \left[\frac{(1.05)^5 - 1}{0.05\,(1.05)^5} \right] = 10\,391$$

that is a sum available for immediate investments of £10 391 against the future annual payments available from rents.

The reverse situation is the recovery of a loan with interest, the latter to be charged only on the amount outstanding–*capital recovery* over a period

$$R = P\left[\frac{i(1+i)^n}{(1+i)^n - 1}\right]$$

EXAMPLE 10.4

A firm sells land for £96 000 and wishes to apply it to a 5 year programme of renovation. The idea is to preserve a listed building and provide new offices. The money can be placed on deposit over the period at an agreed interest of 11 per cent. Then

$$R = 96\,000\left[\frac{0.11\,(1.11)^5}{(1.11)^5 - 1}\right]$$

and thus the sum will support an annual programme of £25 975.

It is not possible to anticipate more than a few applications of the valuation procedures discussed, but one which does arise is the choice between renting or hiring and buying. In the one case payments do not add to the net worth of the firm; in the other, however, the money has to come from capital.

EXAMPLE 10.5

A firm is paying £80 000 p.a. for the rent, external maintenance and heating of offices. £5500 is the average cost of interior decoration and repairs year by year over the last three years. A building on the site next to its out-of-town depot is being offered freehold for £340 000. Moving out of town would save rates to the extent of £2350 p.a. An increased service of company cars is estimated to introduce new costs of £12 000 p.a. Removal would cost £5000.

The cost of heating and maintenance from the audited accounts of the vendor firm is £28 000. The surveyor estimates that at current prices some £9000 will have to be spent on the roof, possibly in 10 years, and that provision should be made for a £15,000 job on the heating system in 15 years.

These sums are reduced to present-worth figures. The life of the building is taken to be 40 years, when it is assumed that the site would be redeveloped. The current site value is put at £80 000. The firm feels that a return on capital used for this purpose would be satisfactory at 10 per cent.

Present worth of lump sums

£340 000 now	£340 000
5000 now	5000
9000 in ten years	
$= \dfrac{9000}{(1.1)^{10}}$	$= 3470$
15 000 in 15 years	
$= \dfrac{15\,000}{(1.1)^{15}}$	$= \dfrac{3591}{£352\,061}$
80 000 in 40 years	
$= \dfrac{80\,000}{(1.1)^{40}}$	$= 1767$ (income)

Present worth of annual sums

$$P = R\left[\frac{(1+i)^n - 1}{i(1+i)^n}\right]$$

Old building   £80 000 + 5500 + 2350 = 87 850
New building   £28 000 + 12 000   = 40 000

Cost of present building   £859 089
Cost of new building   £391 162 + 352 061 − 1767 = £741 456

The balance favours purchase.

The general perceivable trends consequent on such a decision are

(1)   that the annual cost subject to upward revision under pressure of inflation (suggested by an interest rate of 10%) is halved;

(2)   that effective measures to control inflation would reduce interest rates but, by encouraging investment and prosperity, could act against downward adjustment of rents.

The example assumes the availability of capital. It may be raised by a 'rights issue' of shares—an offer to sell authorised but unissued shares, firstly to shareholders and any surplus to the market.

Alternatively a loan may have to be raised. Suppose that a loan is raised at 14 per cent over a period not exceeding 25 years, for which, instead of a 10 per cent return over 40 years, repayments would be

$$R = P\left[\frac{i(1+i)^n}{(1+i)^n - 1}\right] = 345\,000\left[\frac{0.14\,(1.14)^{25}}{(1.14)^{25} - 1}\right] = £50\,197 \text{ p.a.}$$

With £40 000 of annual payments already identified for the new building this means £90 197 p.a. for 25 years and £40 000 for the remainder, or £40 000 p.a. for 40 years with a £50 197 surcharge for the first 25. As we are now concerned with the company's rate of return these give a present worth of £391 162 + 455 640, to which we *add* £5000 + 3470 + 3591 and *deduct* £1767, to arrive at a figure of £857 096. This must be compared with the present worth of annual payments on the present building of £859 089: the comparison evidently remains favourable.

Perpetuity

Before moving on to equivalent annual cost methods of comparison we should discuss long-period returns.

The formula for capital recovery was

$$R = P\left[\frac{i(1+i)^n}{(1+i)^n - 1}\right]$$

which can be written in the form

$$R = P\left[\frac{i}{(1+i)^n - 1} + i\right]$$

This can be checked by writing $X = (1+i)^n$

$$\frac{i}{X-i} + i = \frac{i + i(X-1)}{X-1} = \frac{iX}{X-1} = \frac{i(1+i)^n}{(1+i)^n - 1}$$

Now, as n increases the denominator becomes large in relation to i, and the expression approaches Pi. Therefore, over a long period

$$R = Pi$$

Thus at 10 per cent

$$R = 0.1P$$

and at 8 per cent

$$R = 0.08P$$

The reciprocal of these expressions is the 'years' purchase'—the number of years in which the principal is covered by repayments of interest: for 8 per cent (0.08), 12.5 years; for 15 per cent.(0.1), 10 years; for 12.5 per cent (0.125), 8 years.

In fact the difference between repayments over extended periods of 40, 60, 100 years, etc., and repayments over perpetuity is insignificant. Table 10.1 sets out some of these repayments as values of R/P for rates of 5, 10 and 15 per cent.

Table 10.1

Interest rate (%)	Period in years			
	40	60	100	∞
5	0.0583	0.0528	0.0504	0.05
10	0.1023	0.1003	0.1000(1)	0.1
15	0.1506	0.1500(3)	0.1500	0.15

EXAMPLE 10.6

A builder cannot raise enough capital to bid for a housing site and also to develop it. He expects to be allowed to build 60 dwellings. He considers that a ground rent of £25 p.a. would not deter buyers at his price. He persuades a local charity that has just received a legacy to bid for the lot. Local authority loans are available for up to 5 years at 12 per cent. What ceiling would be put on any bid?

At 12% $R = 0.12P$, and thus $P = 8.3R$.

R_{max} is   £25 × 60   = £1500

Thus P_{max} is

$$8.3 \times 1500 = £12\,500$$

and this is the limiting bid for a 12 per cent rate of return.

Equivalent Annual Cost

When comparisons based on capital involve large sums and the life of the assets concerned is somewhat speculative, some gain in intelligibility may be obtained by expressing the comparative value in terms of annual value (rent rather than purchase price). This is simply an inversion of the formulae and should not affect the conclusions. It is perhaps best illustrated by reworking example 10.5.

The Annual costs already established are as follows

Present building £87 850

New building   £40 000

Turning to the annual value of capital sums, the capital recovery for the new building only is £345 000 at 10 per cent over 40 years

$$R = 345\,000 \left[\frac{0.1\,(1.1)^{40}}{(1.1)^{40} - 1} \right] = 35\,279$$

To this must be added sinking fund payments to cover amounts of

£9000 in 10 years   £565

£15 000 in 15 years £472

There remains the deduction to offset the residual site value

£80 000 in 40 years

$$R = P \left[\frac{i}{(1 + i)^n - 1} \right] = £181$$

The total is

£40 000 + 35 279 + 565 + 472 − 181 = £76 135

The conclusion is again in favour of purchase.

    If, however, we have to recover the £345 000 at 14% over 25 years, that is, £50 197 p.a., we have

£50 197 + 40 000 + 565 + 472 − 181 = £91 053 p.a.

for 25 years, and

40 000 + 565 + 472 − 181 = £40 856 p.a.

for the 15 years remaining. Converting to present worth and calculating a single annual value we get £87 449 p.a., which remains favourable in comparison with the current annual payments of £87 850.

Discounted Cash Flow

To evaluate a situation relating to investment and return by taking into account the time value of money we assume that it is necessary to exchange future sums for present payments. A creditor, having the use of his money before he would otherwise have it, will accept less than the face value of the amount. A debtor, offering early repayment, affords a sum that can earn interest, and would expect to pay less than the face value of the amount. The process is called 'discounting'.

    Almost any enterprise requires periodic payments to set up and maintain it. It also benefits from income. If at the end of a period the outgoings exceed the income then the cash flow is *negative,* but if income exceeds outgoings it is *positive.* For a period of activity each of these can be assigned a present worth, and for two possible courses or more there is a basis for comparing financial performance.

    Simplistic comparisons are sometimes made on some other than a time-value-related basis. The 'payback' method records the time in which the capital sum is recovered in interest or return, after which it implies that any profit is good. The 'yield' is the percentage return based on the average periodic return as a proportion of the capital sum. The percentage rate of return on invested capital can be variously calculated depending firstly on the particular figure for profit that is used. Gross profit, net profit and profit before and after various forms of recovery may be used. That of a single year in an enterprise of longer duration may be untypical. Capital in turn may represent both fixed assets which are deployed for use in the enterprise and working capital, and these are not consistent over time. Assets may have value at the end of the period and an average may be appropriate. Working capital may only have to be provided from other sources for a limited period. However such values are selected, figure 10.1 gives a figure for the yield from such an investment.

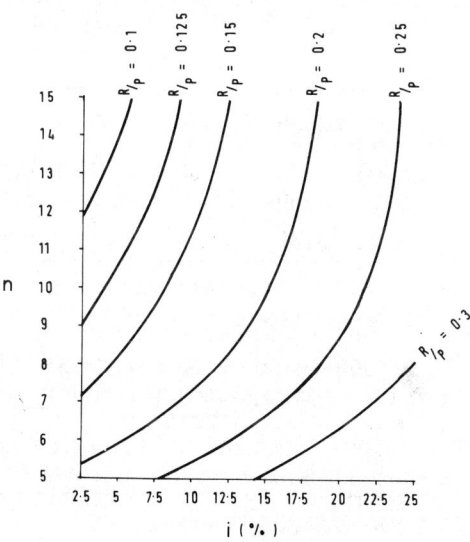

Figure 10.1

It is a feature of U.K. forms of contract that the contractor finances the early stages of the contract. His capital is locked up and thereby made available to the client. It is appropriate that it should earn an adequate return.

The amount concerned has been described in terms of CAPTIM (capital × time). It represents the area of negative cash flow first seen in figure 1.7 and frequently evident thereafter. It is in units of £ months. To estimate the area it is enough to assume a uniform time interval and multiply this by the sum of the negative mid-ordinates.

If we are dealing with 50 000 £ months and the firm requires a 12 per cent p.a. return, then 12 per cent p.a. is 1 per cent per month, and we require to recover £500 per month.

Regular payments (R) to repay capital (P) with interest over n periods are obtained from

$$R = P\left[\frac{i(1 + i)^n}{(1 + i)^n - 1}\right]$$

R/P is evidently equal to the term in square brackets.

Figure 10.1 permits i to be derived from n and R/P.

EXAMPLE 10.7

An item of plant cost £17 000. Running costs are £10 000 p.a. for the first 4 years, and £12 000 for up to 4 years thereafter; a major overhaul or replacement will then have to be considered. It is quite possible that the machine will be obsolete by then and of little value.

The unmodified machine is forecast to return annual amounts of £15 550, 16 500, 16 500, 16 000, 15 500, 15 500 and 14 000. However, by spending an extra £1500 it can complete the job in one year less, returning £16 500, 17 500, 17 500, 17 000, 15 000 and 13 500. The company expects to get 12% on capital.

Nil	15 500	16 500	16 500	16 000	15 500	15 500	14 000
−17 000	−10 000	−10 000	−10 000	−10 000	−12 000	−12 000	−12 000
Balance	+5500	6500	6500	6000	3500	3500	2000
Present worth	4910	5181	4627	2813	1986	1773	905

The present worth is $S/(1 + i)^n$ and the total of the present-worth values of the cash flow is $4910 + 5181 + 4627 + 3813 + 1986 + 1773 + 905 - 17\,000 = + £6195$.

The total income is $5500 + 6500 + 6500 + 6000 + 3500 + 3500 + 2000 = 33\,500$. Averaging over seven years gives £4786; this is the value of R.

The £17 000 capital is recovered in the first three years with £1500 surplus.

Now $R/P = 4786/17000 = 0.28$, and $n = 7$; hence from figure 10.1, $i = 21.5$. Introducing the modification leads to the following values.

Nil	16 500	17 500	17 500	17 000	15 000	14 000
−18 500	−10 000	−10 000	−10 000	−10 000	−12 000	−12 000
Balance	+6500	7500	7500	7000	3000	2000
Present worth	5804	5979	5338	4449	1702	760

The present-worth values of cash flow are $5804 + 5979 + 5338 + 4449 + 1702 + 760 - 18\,500 = £5532$. This is *not* so favourable.

However, the capital is recovered in the first three years but with a surplus of £3000, and so 'payback' would give a different answer.

The total income is the same and thus the average income (R) is £5583; $n = 6$. The £18 500 capital gives $R/P = 5583/18\,500 = 0.3$, and from figure 10.1 $i = 18.75$, which again is less favourable.

It can be seen that using different indices of performance in comparisons may lead to a different result. The more exact methods require little additional effort. However, there are inherent uncertainties in the data, which for forecasting purposes are estimated. Inflation can alter the numerical magnitude of return, and can influence fluctuations in interest rates. Therefore, before accepting the outcome of a comparison it is prudent to review the criteria on which calculations have been based. For both future payments and allowances for depreciation it is possible to devise formulae that provide for uniform changes in rates; however, some simplifying assumption has to be made regarding the trends of change, and reality could be very different.

Trimble (1976) has demonstrated that the rate of inflation, the level and incidence of taxation and the manner in which resources are obtained all interact so as to make choice in this business situation anything but clear. The decision to buy or hire, for instance, may be different depending on whether or not the rate of inflation exceeds the going rate of interest. The best time at which to replace plant may be equally unclear. Loughborough University of Technology has thus programmed the associated calculations in order that the power of a computer may be applied to such decisions.

The interest rate that corresponds to the discounted cash flow over the period concerned is 30.9 per cent in respect of £6195 gained in 7 years on a principal of £17 000; for £5532 gained in 6 years on a principal of £18 500 it is reduced to 19.8 per cent.

This would be the rate that would recover the amounts of positive cash flow in order to balance cost and income.

Raising Finance

When funds are needed it is possible to approach a finance house, which might offer funds on mortgage. The firm must then put up assets as a security. Both interest and capital repayments must be paid regularly, and there is provision for fluctuation of the rate of interest. We have been dealing with repayments of a similar kind.

Other methods of attracting funds trade on some measure of expectation rather than assurance of return. The bigger the risk, the higher the rate of return that will be offered. Bonds can be issued, each with some face value and rate of interest stated. Such debentures take preference over distributed profits. For a firm to pass over payment would be an invitation to the market to react sharply. It would afford bad publicity, and creditors would regard it as an invitation to press for payment. To keep down the dividend rate it is possible to offer conversion to ordinary shares after a time (when the capital has presumably increased the firm's net worth), or to offer the bonds at a discount. Once the issue is on the market, its value changes with the general financial situation and the firm's performance, and it may be necessary to pay a premium to get the bonds.

EXAMPLE 10.8

£100 debentures paying $2\frac{1}{2}$ per cent per quarter are offered at £97. The money is repayable in 20 years (not, as for loans on mortgage, in the course of the period of loan).

A single bond will cost £97.00

$$present worth = -97$$

80 payments of £2.50

$$present worth = +2.50 \left[\frac{1.025^{80} - 1}{0.025(1.025)^{80}} \right]$$

$$= 86.13$$

Repayment

$$present\ worth = +\frac{100}{1.025^{80}}$$

$$= +13.87$$

$$86.13 + 13.87 - 97 = +3$$

The effective return is greater than 2.5 per cent.
Try 3 per cent; this gives similar values except for i

$$75.50 + 9.40 - 97 = -12.10$$

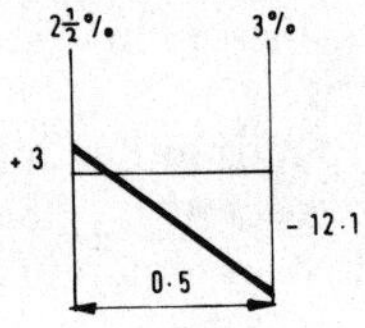

Figure 10.2

Interpolating, the effective yield is

$$2.5 + 0.5\left[\frac{3}{3 + 12.10}\right] = 2.6$$

Thus the purchaser gets 2.6 per cent return.

Let us assume that to raise £20 000 in this way costs the firm £1200 in fees and charges; from the firm's point of view the interest calculations take the following form
Net increase in funds £18 800

$$present\ worth = +18\ 800$$

Interest

$$present\ worth = -2.5 \times 200\left[\frac{1.025^{80} - 1}{0.025(1.025)^{80}}\right]$$

$$= -17\ 226$$

Repayment

$$present\ worth = \frac{-20\ 000}{1.025^{80}}$$

$$= -2774$$

$$18\ 800 - (17\ 226 + 2774) = -1200$$

The firm is effectively paying more than 2.5 per cent.

Try 3 per cent changing only i in the above calculations

$$1800 - (15\ 100 + 1880) = +1920$$

Interpolating, the effective interest rate is

$$2.5 + 0.5 \left[\frac{1200}{1200 + 1920} \right]$$

$$= 2.7$$

Thus the firm pays 2.7 per cent

Payments are quarterly and the equivalent annual rate of £2.6 paid on each £100 bond at such intervals is 10.8 per cent while that of £2.7 paid out on each £100 bond quarterly is 11.25 per cent.

Lesser degrees of security are then available by the issue of stock against expectations of profit. Expectations of benefit can be offered in a bewildering variety of forms. Preference shares that have priority in any distribution of profit may be convertible after a period into ordinary shares, may be entitled to retrospective payment of dividend should any payment be passed and may even entitle the holders to some supplementary payment from distributed profits in good years. They are offered on a prospectus which determines the conditions and, in particular, this should state the rate of interest and the term (if any) within which the principal sum is redeemable. As there may well be less than complete certainty of the amount and timing of return, the use of discounted cash flow techniques must become more speculative.

Again, as was mentioned earlier, a firm may offer authorised but unissued shares—a 'rights issue'. This raises capital by requiring the shareholders to take up unissued shares or dilute the ownership.

The Business Environment

Business must react to changes in the law, to political pressures and to changes in the socioeconomic climate, however these may arise. The market for finance itself reacts to the *probability* of such changes as much as to their eventuality. In the face of checks and restraints applied through company law and legislative provision for taxation a firm seeks to match financial needs to what is currently the most attractive way of raising funds. We should, perhaps, firstly discuss the influence of company law.

The character of firms in the United Kingdom is controlled in a number of ways by their legal definition. The degree and distribution of liability for the business behaviour of the firm relates to restraints upon fund raising, matters of disclosure of information, tenure as a business and the manner in which taxation is levied.

Firms with unlimited liability may belong to a single proprietor, to a partnership or to a company. The more partners, the greater the dilution of ownership, which affects both taxation and the power to borrow. A division of profits being a usual feature of any partnership agreement, it follows that a single proprietor faced with surtax may find it preferable to gain funds from a sleeping partner or the contribution of a working one in return for profit, some of which might otherwise have been lost to the Inland Revenue. Parting with the satisfaction of sole ownership may aid the retention of profit within the business and make more working capital available.

An unlimited company has a degree of freedom in the issue and transfer of shares that is denied to limited liability companies. It costs less to set up such a company. Liability for debts is divided in proportion to that share of the equity held. There is no limitation on the number of such holdings nor can shareholders be sued individually. Shareholders acquire voting as well as dividend rights. The company has flexibility in its ability to trade in its shares and to change the nature of equity, but the lack of accountability tends to discourage public subscription.

The responsibility for debts in the case of owners of a limited liability company extends no further than the fully paid-up value of the shares held, provided that no other monetary obligations have been agreed. Creditors can seek repayment no further than the firm itself. There must be at least seven shareholders, but there is no upper limit. Any amount of the subscription remaining on call, where shares are not fully paid up, may be forfeit.

Unlimited companies centre all rights, responsibilities and duties on the partners. Each is an agent for all, and they are jointly and severally liable for debts incurred by the firm. On the death of a partner the partnership terminates. Unless circumvented by suitable agreements that reconstitute the firm the value of its property is realised for taxation purposes. A partner may not assign the right of management except by agreement. There are upper limits on the number of partners. There is no Memorandum of Association as for a limited company, and thus the direction of the enterprise is not constrained. A partnership need neither publish and deposit accounts nor convene shareholders' meetings.

Taxation does not bear evenly, nor over time consistently, on the two main types of firm. Its incidence is a matter of politics. At different times, therefore, there are different pressures upon companies to change their status.

Limited companies, if incorporated, are termed public companies even if no public subscription is involved. Being limited in both the transfer of its shares and in its membership a private company may find it difficult to raise capital funds. On the other hand shares can be transferred with little formality and, within the limitations, fund raising is inexpensive.

Partnerships are taxed according to each partner's share of the firm's net profit. In recent years high earnings have attracted punitive rates of taxation. Therefore, in order to pursue a programme of growth, and to plough back profits for the purpose, firms have been placed under some pressure to 'go public'.

Closed companies, being those under the control of five or fewer participating owners, who may be individuals, a trust or group of individuals, tend to face more severe taxation than firms of more dilute ownership. Control in the above sense means holding more than half of the equity. Whereas a public company can reinvest or distribute its profits, a closed company finds its owners taxed again on distributed earnings. The mechanism is not important, and change can be introduced at any time, but it is one of the pressures now inclining the small company toward simple partnership and the large one to public-company status.

Companies have an advantage if they are able to attract funds free of association with the ownership of specific assets. Once a mortgage is attached to some set of assets, changes that affect value can only be made with the lender's permission. It is an advantage to be able to invite public subscription to an issue of shares or debentures. Such facilities are restricted in the case of private companies, and do not apply to partnerships. The latter borrow on mortgage or on promissory notes and are solely dependent upon the attitude of the lender. However, whereas for public companies response is largely influenced by financial statements, periodically published, in the case of a partnership response may be influenced by the wealth, skill, standing and integrity of the partners.

A 'sleeping partner' may negotiate a placement of funds for a share of the proceeds under terms of limited liability. A working partner must accept unlimited liability. A partnership can thus raise money at nominal cost, often at the expense of some dilution of ownership. A company can raise funds without doing so but must seek the services of

(1)   a stockbroker, who introduces the company to
(2)   an issuing house, which advises on and manages the issue and arranges for Stock Exchange quotation;
(3)   an underwriter, who, for a fee, guarantees the sale of all the shares at a given price; and
(4)   the Stock Exchange, which provides a market quotation.

Fees are payable at all stages, but the system guarantees the firm capital under the agreed terms at an agreed rate.

Companies can issue nonvoting shares, preference shares and debentures, none of which dilute ownership. The compensatory assurances and benefits may, however, have to be greater than those of shares that offer participation in any gain in the worth of the firm resulting from the employment of the funds obtained. There are may variations of risk, assurance and reward. The manner in which shares are placed varies from offers by tender to an offer made directly to an institution, which will hold them as an investment. The complexities are such that advice based on familiarity with the market can hardly be ignored.

Where a company pursues liquidity to the point that it maintains a large balance of idle cash, fails to manage the volume and recovery of debt and/or fails to exploit the growth potential of its market, then it signals its candidature for takeover. Construction contractors are often so involved with contract cost control—probably because their experience is rather in this than in other areas of management—that they pay less attention than they might to the management of finance. However, the best use of their prime enabling resource should be a matter of concern if not of expertise.

References

Trimble, E. G., *The Effect of Inflation on Plant-Costs and Replacement Policies.* Paper to the Institute of Building Seminar on the Threat of Insolvency (January 16, 1976).

Twitty, R., *Measuring Financial Liquidity in British Construction Firms,* M.Sc. Dissertation (Department of Construction and Environmental Health, University of Aston, Birmingham, 1977).

Index